*H*is *B*anner over Me Is *Love*

More Dynamic Banner Designs for Worship Settings

by
Dale A. Bargmann

SAINT LOUIS

To my family and friends for their continuing support.

Unless otherwise noted, Scripture quotations are taken from THE HOLY BIBLE, NEW INTERNATIONAL VER-
SION®. Copyright © 1973, 1978, 1984 by the International Bible Society. Used by permission of Zon-
dervan Publishing House. All rights reserved.

The "NIV" and "New International Version" trademarks are registered in the United States Patent and
Trademark Office by International Bible Society. Use of either trademark requires the permission of the International Bible Society.

Scripture quotations marked RSV are from the Revised Standard Version of the Bible, copyrighted 1946,
1952, © 1971, 1973. Used by permission.

Copyright © 1995 Concordia Publishing House
3558 S. Jefferson Avenue, St. Louis, MO 63118-3968
Manufactured in the United States of America

Library of Congress Cataloging-in-Publication Data.

Bargmann, Dale, 1947 –
    His banner over me is love : more dynamic designs for worship settings / Dale A. Bargmann.
      p.   cm.
    ISBN 0-570-04818-4
    1. Church pennants. 2. Christian art and symbolism. I. Title.
BV168.F5B36   1995
246′.55—dc20   95-11376

1 2 3 4 5 6 7 8 9 10   04 03 02 01 00 99 98 97 96 95

Contents

Preface

In ancient times monarchs and generals used banners as signals to rally troops in battle. They would erect them on a hill for all to see and in the case of the Roman army call attention to them with the sound of a trumpet.

A number of references to banners are found in the Old Testament. Though few in number, they attest to the significance of banners in the history of God's first chosen people. The earliest, Ex. 17:15, states that "Moses built an altar (to commemorate the Israelites victory over the Amalekites) and called it The LORD is my Banner." Centuries later Isaiah announced in reference to the coming Messiah: "In that day the Root of Jesse will stand as a banner for the peoples; the nations will rally to him and his place of rest will be glorious … He will raise a banner for the nations and gather the exiles of Israel" (Is. 11:10, 12). Then there is the passage that provided the title for this book, Song of Songs 2:4: "He has taken me to the banquet hall, and his banner over me is love." Clearly, in Old Testament times banners were more than mere decorative cloth hangings. They inspired the people, rallied them for action and, most importantly, they signified the presence of God.

With such superlatives in mind it is time to evaluate and ask questions: Do we utilize banners to create an atmosphere conducive to worship? If so, do they reveal and reinforce the message of the Gospel? Do they elevate the spirit, provoke thought or incite action? Do they generate any kind of response? Are there people within our community of faith blessed with artistic ability whose talents go unutilized? Well designed and crafted banners can transform any nos to these questions into emphatic yeses.

As visual hymns of praise, banners can lend beauty and life to your worship experiences, point to the reality of the Gospel message, and work together with music and the spoken and written word to build up the body of Christ. I offer these banner designs and accompanying guidelines and explanations in the hope that they will help you reach these high goals.

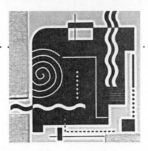

Gathering Necessary Items

Design Notebook: It is a good idea to have a loose-leaf binder with filler paper handy at all times, to keep procedural notes, lists of supplies, fabric swatches, color ideas, and copies of banner designs for reference.

CONSTRUCTION TOOLS AND MATERIALS

Most of the tools and materials needed for constructing the designs in this book are listed below. They are not all necessary for any one design. At the beginning of a banner project, check the instructions first before deciding what to buy.

Cutting Tools

- Scissors—two pairs: one for paper, one reserved for cloth (paper dulls cutting edges).
- X-Acto knife and blades.

Marking Tools

- No. 2 pencils or .7 mm automatic pencils with HB black leads.
- Medium ballpoint pens—black and blue.
- Eagle Prismapastel pencils or Crayola colored pencils in light and dark colors for marking fabric—obtained through craft or art suppliers.
- Wooden stick ($3/4'' \times 3/4'' \times 3'$) to serve as a makeshift compass for drawing large circles and arcs. For a pivot, drill a $1/4''$ hole near one end and insert a pencil, eraser end down. Use a small C-clamp to secure another pencil, point down, to the other end. The C-clamp allows for adjustment to any needed radius.
- Circle templates, small compass, or French curves—aids for drawing curves and circles.

Obtained through hobby, art, or drafting suppliers.

Paper for Patterns

- Tissue gift-wrapping paper (similar in weight to that used for dressmaker's patterns).
- Butcher paper.
- Brown wrapping paper.
- Newspaper, especially the classified ads.
- Wide rolls of wrapping paper, particularly those with the pattern printed only on one side.

Bonding Materials

- Scotch Magic tape (green package).
- Scotch removable tape (blue package), or Scotch Safe Release masking tape.
- Double-stick tape.
- Masking tape.
- Elmer's Glue-All—general purpose white glue, best with cotton and cotton blends.
- Sobo Glue by Delta, Aleene's Tacky Glue—white craft glues suitable for fabrics.
- Pellon Wonder-Under, Aleene's Fusible Web, and Therm O Web Heat-n-Bond—iron-on adhesives with paper backing: 17″ wide; purchased in bulk from cloth suppliers.
- Stitch Witchery— 3/4″ wide iron-on bonding web for linings and hems.
- Glue sticks.
- Velcro hook and loop strips, and Velcro adhesive (1 oz. tube)—for bonding.

Miscellaneous

- Plastic fishing-tackle box—for storing tools and small supplies.

- Opaque projector or overhead transparency projector.
- Ball-head straight pins.
- Lightweight pressing cloth—for protecting fabrics from direct contact with iron (a piece of 100% cotton muslin, a cotton dish towel, or an old bedsheet).
- Carpenter's square—L-shaped with 18" and 24" sides, or a large T-square.
- Yardstick.
- 12' retractable tape measure.
- 12" rule—preferably clear plastic.
- Iron and ironing board.
- Sewing machine and sewing needle with a selection of threads in colors to match fabrics being used.
- Wright's bias tape, double or single fold—for finishing raw fabric edges.
- Inexpensive paint brushes—1/2" and 1 1/2".

Hanging Supplies

- Hammer, screwdriver, and pliers.
- Drill, electric or push type, with bits.
- 4d smooth box nails, or similar.
- S- or 8-hooks (so named because of their shape).
- 3/4" dowels—lengths as needed.
- Lock seam or adjustable spring-pressure curtain rods, purchased at cloth or decorating suppliers.
  (All the above items are available through hardware suppliers.)
- Drapery weights.
- Fishing line—15 lb., or higher, test.

Special Purpose Materials

- For outlining: Crayola or Kodak washable markers (purchased in sets from craft suppliers); permanent felt-tip markers (regular tip, in black, and other colors as needed); fluorescent highlighters; yarns (4 ply, 100% acrylic); embroidery paints (preferably the puff type in various colors).
- Acrylic paints, 2 fl. oz. tubes, Liquitex, Hyplar,

or Windsor Newton brand—from art or hobby suppliers.
- Spray paint (12 oz. can) or a can of quick-drying enamel, preferably red.

FABRIC CHOICES

Pick a fabric supplier with a large selection. There are many attractive fabrics suitable for making banners, but some types work better than others. Generally speaking, 100% cottons and cotton blends work best. Avoid stretchy knits (especially 100% polyesters) and those with loose weaves or heavy textures.

Recommended Fabrics

Broadcloth—100% cotton or polyester-cotton blend; 45" wide; relatively inexpensive; excellent color range, but lighter shades do not cover as well as darker ones.

Cotton sheeting—100% cotton; 60" wide; heavier than broadcloth; covers well.

Felt—100% acrylic or polyester; 72" wide; smooth surface; good color range and intensity; good as a background material: it is economical, readily available, nonfraying, and does not require lining (although lining does add stability).

Flannel—100% cotton (avoid polyester); 45" wide; limited number of solid colors available; easy to glue; accepts paint well (see "Learning Useful Techniques").

Interlock knits—polyester-cotton or polyester-rayon blend; 60" wide; nonfraying; good color range.

Muslin—100% cotton; 45"–108" wide; primarily available in white and natural unbleached, also in a number of solid colors; light in weight with a smooth finish; covers well and works well with paints and markers.

Polished apple solids—polyester-cotton blend; 45" wide; covers well; good color range with slight sheen.

Poplin—cotton-polyester blend; 45" wide; heavier and more opaque than broadcloth; good for backgrounds, if lined.

Robe velour—60" wide; 80% acetate/20%

nylon; gives a plush look similar to velvet, but without the weight; nonfraying; good for backgrounds; also good for lettering on selected designs.

Trigger cloth—60″ wide; available only in black, white, and basic colors; a good background material on selected designs because of its weight and smooth texture; needs to be lined.

Check sale tables for remnants and mis-dyed lots. Do not be afraid to mix materials. Plan to use heavier fabrics (felt, poplin, trigger cloth) for backgrounds and lighter fabrics (flannel, broadcloth) for design elements. Also try drapery and upholstery fabrics for backgrounds, but avoid those with heavy or rough textures, or all-over patterns.

Specialty Fabrics

Lycra—60% Lycra/40% nylon; relatively expensive; available in several good bright colors, including fluorescents.

Solid taffeta—100% polyester; 60″ wide; good for processional banners.

Lining Materials

Drapery lining—48″ wide; poly-cotton blend.
Fusible interfacing—22″ and 45″ widths.

Sale and remnant tables are a good source of heavy fabrics to use for linings. Extra-wide drapery and upholstery materials, suitable for backing large banners, can often be found at reduced prices as well.

FULL-SIZE DESIGNS

Enlarging the Designs

Pattern Method
The best way to enlarge designs is to use an opaque projector. This allows the image to be cast directly from the page in the book. Next best is to use an overhead transparency projector, most likely available from the church office. Its biggest advantage is that the design can be scaled to a size that fits the dimensions of the display area. To use an overhead projector, first use a copier to transfer the design in the book to a clear acetate sheet.

1. Project the design onto a smooth wall at eye level. Adjust the image to the desired size by moving the projector toward or away from the wall, measuring with a 12′ rule. Turn the projector off.

2. Prepare the sheet of paper that will serve as the full-size pattern by cutting it to the exact size of the finished banner. Make sure all sides are square. This is an important step if the finished banner is to hang properly, because the pattern will be used both for cutting the design pieces and for sizing the background.

3. Turn on the projector and tape the blank pattern paper to the wall within the image area. Use removable tape to prevent wall damage. *Make sure the image is square with the paper.*

4. Trace the design lines in pencil (a marker can bleed through the paper) taking special care with the lettering. Keep a rule handy for straight lines, and a compass, French curve, or circle template for curves.

5. Block the projected image in sections to check for missed lines. Look carefully at the lettering again and make sure that the lines are plumb with each other.

6. Turn off the projector, and, before removing the pattern from the wall, do a final check for any untraced elements.

7. To aid reassembly after cutting, number each of the shapes and indicate its color. Transfer the numbers to the corresponding shapes on the original in the book. Also, to prevent pieces from being accidently placed upside down, indicate the top of each with a *T*.

8. Set the pattern aside. Do not cut it apart yet. It needs to be kept whole for some of the next steps.

Have a second sheet of paper handy as some of the designs contain overlapping design elements that require separate tracings.

If projection transparencies are unavailable, make 2 copies of the chosen design onto plain paper. Carefully cut out the de-

sign elements and, with double-stick tape, attach them to the glass bed of the projector. Proceed as above, except now you will be tracing shadows of the shapes.

No-Pattern Method

For simple designs with few overlapping elements, consider projecting the design directly onto the cloth pieces, skipping the paper pattern altogether.

1. Project the design directly onto a wall.

2. Use a 12′ tape measure to size the image to the exact size of the finished banner.

3. Attach the cloth pieces to the wall over the image area with safe-release masking tape.

4. Trace the design areas with clearly contrasting pastel pencils or colored pencils onto the fabrics for the banner.

5. Cut out the pieces just inside the pencil lines as the lines might otherwise show on the finished banner.

Estimating Fabric Needs

Background—to determine the amount of background material needed, start with the dimensions of the finished banner. Then:

• add 2″ to the *length* to compensate for cutting error, plus 3″ for each hem.

• add 2″ to the *width* to compensate for cutting error, plus 2″ for hems or sewn-in linings (not necessary if lining with fusible interfacing or other materials bonded with Stitch Witchery).

• add another 2″ to both *length* and *width* to compensate for shrinkage from prewashing (not necessary for upholstery fabrics or felt, which do not require preshrinking).

• add extra yardage to allow for experimentation with unfamiliar materials and processes.

Lining—Purchase enough to cover the background piece plus a little extra.

Fabrics for design elements—use the full-size pattern to make rough measurements of lettering and color areas. Do not scrimp. Allow for error and experimentation. These measurements will also determine the amount of iron-on adhesive to purchase, if it is being used to attach the design pieces to the background.

When making estimates, remember that most fabrics, with the exception of those noted above, are manufactured in 45" widths.

Putting the Banner Together

PREPARATIONS

For assembly, it is best to work in a well-lit area on a table large enough to handle the full-size banner. It is also possible to use a carpeted floor, or any space, where the banner can be left undisturbed until completed.

To prevent puckering and uneven bonding, fabrics (except felt and upholstery materials) must be preshrunk and pressed smooth. Preshrinking is especially important for 100% cotton and cotton blends because it removes the sizing or starch that can interfere with bonding. Preshrink the fabrics by putting them through a complete wash and dry cycle. Be sure to check fabric care instructions at the time of purchase. As with regular laundering, light and dark fabrics need to be separated.

Background

Materials

• Carpenter's square, or T-square
• 12″ rule
• Pastel pencils, or Crayola colored pencils (light or dark, to contrast with fabric color)
• Straight pins
• Sharp cloth scissors

Procedure

1. Lay background cloth *wrong* side up on the work surface and place the carefully squared pattern on top.

2. Align pattern edges with the fabric weave and secure with several straight pins.

3. Use the pattern to measure cutting lines, with allowances for finishing. Add 2 1/2″–3″ to the length for each pole loop. Add less to the bottom if using drapery weights. If the lining is to be sewn to the back, add 1″ to the width for seams. Disregard if the sides are to be left as cut edges (as on felt), or if the lining is to be bonded to the back.

4. Apply fray-check along the cutting lines to prevent edges from unraveling after cutting (unnecessary with felt).

Design Pieces

The pattern pieces need to be cut out. Stack them, as work proceeds, according to the color fabric they will be used on later. Set the larger background pieces aside for use as positioning templates during the process of final assembly.

Before tracing the pattern pieces onto their respective fabrics, a method for attaching the fabric design pieces to the background of the banner needs to be determined.

The least expensive method is gluing. White glue is easiest to use with fabrics. Of the ordinary brands on the market, the best is Elmer's Glue-All. It is heavy enough in consistency not to soak in too quickly; its applicator tip delivers a smooth, even flow; and it has demonstrated its capacity to hold banners together even through years of continuous use.

Also suitable for fabrics, though more expensive, are craft glues such as Sobo Glue by Delta and Aleene's Tacky Glue. All dry clear but have several disadvantages. They can cause moisture-sensitive fabrics to pucker if not preshrunk first; they can bleed through thinner fabrics, leaving a shiny discoloration; and they do not work well with polyester.

An alternative to gluing is the use of highly-recommended iron-on adhesives like Pellon Wonder-Under, Aleene's Fusible Web, or Therm O Web Heat-n-Bond. They can be purchased in both prepackaged amounts or off the bolt by the yard. Though somewhat more expensive than gluing, they bring several advantages to the banner-making process. They

- are easier and faster to use than glue.
- leave no mess.
- eliminate frayed edges.
- can be applied in any direction.
- can be dry cleaned or washed.
- are good for fabrics that react adversely to moisture.
- are good with fabrics that do not take glue.

Testing, as always, is the best way to decide on a method. Use 6″ swatches of the materials involved. Try gluing pieces of broadcloth, flannel, and polycotton sheeting to felt (use Elmer's and a craft glue). Make one piece a letter like *S* or *E*. Then bond the same fabrics with squares of fusible web, following the instructions furnished with the material. Allow the samples to cool and dry completely. Be sure, in all cases, to time the procedure. Then compare results:

- Check the edges for fraying and puckering.
- Check for adhesive bleed-through.
- Check to see that the pieces lie flat.
- Check the strength of the bond by trying to pull the pieces apart.

All things considered, the iron-on adhesive usually proves the best. It is more expensive, but this disadvantage seems minor when compared with the time it saves.

ASSEMBLY

To Begin

1. Press the background to remove wrinkles.

2. For reference, mark seam and hem allowances with straight pins placed parallel to the edges and spaced about 12″ apart.

Gluing Method

Materials

- Paper pattern pieces
- Fabrics for design pieces
- Straight pins
- Sharp cloth scissors
- Carpenter's square
- Glues

Procedure

1. Lay all fabrics for the design pieces *right* side up. Position pattern pieces, also *right* side up, on top. Leave about 1/4″ between each piece to be cut. *Align all the letters in the same direction*, that is, on the same grain. Secure all the pattern pieces with straight pins.

2. Cut pieces out using smooth strokes to avoid ragged edges. Check the original design in the book for any abutting elements and cut one 1/4″ larger so that it will fit under the other. Arrange the pieces roughly in position on the background as they are cut.

3. Remove the pins and arrange the pieces in final position using reserved pattern templates as guides. Step back and check for reversed letters and awkward spacing.

4. Prepare for gluing. If the design has overlapping elements, the lower elements need to be attached first. Temporarily set the upper ones aside.

5. Take one element at a time and lay the arm of the carpenter's square across the center of the element to hold it in position. Lift the exposed half of the element away from the background and apply a steady, unbroken line of glue along all edges of its underside. Drop it back into position and press down gently. Repeat with the other shapes until half of each is glued. Let them dry thoroughly, and then glue the other halves using the same method.

6. Reposition any pieces that had to be set aside and repeat the gluing procedure.

7. Allow everything to dry completely before handling further.

Do not discard letter patterns. Put them in large clasp envelopes, record the contents of the envelope on the outside of the envelope, and file the envelope for future projects.

Iron-on Adhesive Method

Materials

- Fabrics for design pieces
- Fusible adhesive to cover
- Straight pins
- Sharp cloth scissors
- Iron and ironing board

Read the instructions that come with the fusible interfacing carefully, and do a test on swatches of the fabrics for each banner.

Procedure

1. Preheat the iron on the dry wool setting (do not use steam).

2. The fabric for the design pieces goes *face down* on the ironing board. Position an adhesive sheet textured side down on top of the fabric.

3. Place the iron on the paper side of the adhesive sheet and press 1–3 seconds *only*. (The object is not to melt the glue, but to transfer it to the back of the fabric.) Let cool.

4. Pin paper pattern pieces *right side* up to the front (cloth side) of the prepared fabrics. It is especially important that letters be aligned in the same direction, that is, on the same grain.

5. Cut the design pieces from the prepared fabric according to the pattern. Remove the pins. Carefully peel off the paper backing and position, adhesive side down, on the background. Use reserved pattern templates as guides.

6. Double-check wording for spelling and reversed or upside down letters. Also check spacing and alignment.

7. Preheat the iron on dry wool setting.

8. Cover an area with a damp pressing cloth and press approximately 10 seconds. Do not slide the iron back and forth. Lift it to the next position, overlapping iron placement to insure complete bonding. *Do not overheat.* (Overheating causes adhesive to migrate back toward the iron.) For large areas, begin fusing in the center and work outward to the sides and corners.

While bonding the design elements, move the banner as little as possible to prevent jostling the arrangement. Place the ironing board adjacent to and level with the work surface and slide the banner onto it for fusing. A sheet of corrugated cardboard also makes a suitable ironing surface if the work surface is the floor. Simply slide the sheet of cardboard under the area to be fused.

FINISHING

Lining

Lining is recommended for practically all banners because it gives added stability when hanging. It is optional for banners with backgrounds of felt and necessary for banners with backgrounds of woven or lightweight fabrics.

Preshrink lining materials, except felt, upholstery, and drapery fabrics by machine washing or pressing with an iron and a wet pressing cloth. To prepare fusible interfacing, dip it in a sink of warm water, lay it flat between bath towels and pat it dry to remove excess moisture. Hang it to air dry.

Method I. Apply a fusible interfacing to the back. Primarily for lightweight fabrics; also poplins, linens, wools, and fabrics with special finishes.

1. Trim the banner to its finished size, allowing an extra 3″ at the top for a pole casing. No allowances are needed for the sides or bottom.

2. Place the banner *face side down* on the work surface. Position the interfacing *rough (adhesive) side down* on top of it. Pin it in place along the edges.

3. Preheat the iron on the wool setting. Baste at a few points along the edges by pressing lightly with the tip of the iron. Remove the pins.

4. Cover the interfacing with a damp pressing cloth and fuse about 15 seconds. Do not slide the iron. Fuse section by section, overlapping the previous area. Let cool.

5. Turn the banner over and repeat the ironing process to achieve a secure bond.

6. Trim any excess lining material.

Method II. Bond a heavy fabric to the back. Primarily for felt and heavier background fabrics.

1. Trim the banner to its finished size, allow 2 1/2″–3″ at the top for a pole casing. No allowances are needed for the sides or bottom.

2. Cut the lining material slightly larger than the banner. Place it wrong side up on the work surface. Position the banner *face side up* on top of it.

3. Preheat the iron at the wool setting.

4. Place strips of Stitch Witchery between the fabric layers along the edges of the banner.

5. Cover with a damp pressing cloth and press along the edges for 10 seconds. *Do not slide the iron.*

6. Turn the banner over and press along the edges for another 10 seconds.

7. Turn the banner over once more and trim any excess lining material.

With either of these methods, the fused edges will, with careful handling, not unravel. However, they can be dressed up with strips of quilt edging in a color to match the background.

Method III. Stabilize edges before lining. For fabrics that unravel easily.

1. Trim the banner to its finished size, allowing 3″ at the top for a pole casing, and allowing 3/4″ at the bottom and each side.

2. Turn the banner *face side down.*

3. Fold the side and bottom edges over, forming 3/4″ hems. Press with the iron to crease and bond to the back of the banner with strips of Stitch Witchery.

4. Cut a lining of heavy cloth slightly smaller than the finished banner and bond it to the background along all the edges with Stitch Witchery.

Method IV. Sew a heavy fabric or drapery lining to the back. An alternate method for felt, and medium and heavyweight fabrics.

1. Trim the banner to its finished size, adding 3″ to the top for a pole casing, and adding 5/8″ to each side and the bottom.

2. Place the lining material *right side up* on the work surface. Place the banner *right side down* on top of it making sure that the grains of the fabrics are aligned.

3. Pin the side and bottom edges together.

4. Set the sewing machine to "straight stretch stitch." Sew the sides and bottom together with a 5/8″ seam leaving the top end open just like a pillow case.

5. Trim the seams and cut the bottom corners off at a 45° angle.

6. Turn the banner and lining *right side out.*

7. Sew or bond the top edges together.

Finishing the Top Edge

The designs in this book work best when hung by inserting a pole through a simple 3″ casing applied at the top. No matter which lining method has been used, all banners can be finished at the top in the same way.

Procedure

1. Turn the banner *face side down*.

2. Mark a line 6″ down from and parallel to the top edge. Fold the top over to meet the line, forming a 3″ casing. Bond with Stitch Witchery.

3. For added security, edge stitch the casing with a sewing machine set on "straight stretch stitch" or with needle and thread using a simple whipstitch.

All methods provide enough stability so that a bottom pole is unnecessary. If the bottom edge should curl or sag, add drapery weights to the lower corners as appropriate.

Outlining Design Elements

Before any banner is hung, it should be thoughtfully appraised from a distance. If the images fail to stand out, or are unclear, simple outlining of one or two of the design elements can be used to bring things into focus.

Fluorescent highlighters (1/4″ wide) add subtle radiance without becoming obtrusive. The best colors are hot pink, yellow, orange, chartreuse, and light blue. Draw lines about 3/16″ wide directly on the background, or on the edge of the elements. Make samples of both to see which works better.

Permanent felt-tip markers (1/4″ tip) in colors contrasting with both the background and the elements being outlined will sharpen definition considerably. For instance, outline a white form set against a dark blue background with an orange marker, or outline a chartreuse form set against a yellow background with a dark green marker. Draw the lines 1/8″–1/4″ wide on the edge of the forms. This technique works best on 100% cottons or cotton blends with a smooth finish.

Yarns (4-ply, 100% acrylic) add the extra dimension of depth and anchor the elements in place. The process can be time consuming, but the results are well worth it. Remember:

• Yarn outlines are best applied after lining.

• Color combinations need to be tested by doing a dry outline first.

• Care should be taken when pressing. (Prolonged exposure to steam can soften the glue and cause the yarn to loosen.)

With these pointers in mind:

1. Slide a sheet of corrugated cardboard under the area to be outlined.

2. With sharp scissors, cut the end of the yarn square and dab it with a bit of glue to prevent unraveling.

3. Outline the shape with an even, unbroken line of white glue about the width of the yarn. Begin at a corner or point, if possible, and lay the yarn gently onto the glue line. Do not pull. Press it in with the fingers.

4. To bend the yarn around corners, secure it with vertical pins stuck down through the strands and into the cardboard.

5. Cut the finishing end of the yarn only after most of the outline is in place.

Fabric paints (puff type) are a good alternative to yarn, especially with fabrics that do not accept glue well. Work quickly to keep the lines uniform. Practice on scraps first. One undesirable quality of fabric paint is its semigloss finish when dry.

Washable marking pens are useful for both outlining and shading and work well on fabrics that are 100% cotton or cotton blends with a smooth finish. Lightly outline the shape with a 1/4″–1/2″ wide line, and then, with an inexpensive 1/2″ watercolor brush, dampen the line and the area immediately around it with tap water. The marker will bleed, creating a subtle color gradation. Allow to dry naturally. For best results, use colors within the same family as that of the shape being outlined, for example, red on pink, violet on lavender, or dark green on chartreuse. A certain amount of daring is required for this procedure, but the results are worth it. Always do a test piece first.

Outlining adds a personal touch to a banner. Like the amen to a prayer, the alleluia at Easter, or the artist's signature on a painting, it signifies completion.

DISPLAY

Improper display can diminish the finished product. Consequently, significant attention should be given to the way in which banners are hung.

Where practical, banners should be hung 3″–6″ away from the wall rather than flush with it. This lends depth and a feeling of life. All efforts should be made to keep hanging methods as unobtrusive as possible. Avoid heavy cords, ropes, or chains. One solution is to suspend the banners from above. Hang two lengths of clear fishing line from the sanctuary ceiling about 3′ apart and 6″ out from the wall. Tie S-hooks to each at the point where the top of the banner will be suspended. (Be sure the points are level with each other.) Drive small 4d box nails into the ends of a 3/4″ dowel the width of the banner. Leave 1/2″ of the nails exposed. Suspend the banner by slipping the nails through the S-hooks. Changing banners is relatively easy with a stepladder, and, because the lines are virtually invisible, they can be left in place when no banner is displayed.

Attached to the Building

Valance curtain rods provide a practical alternative for both seasonal and permanent wall displays. Lengths can be adjusted to fit banners ranging in width from 26″–82″. They are supported by two small brackets, and, of major advantage, project 3″–5 1/2″ (depending on brand) from the wall. Manufacturers include Gold Seal, Graber, and Newell. Adjustable spring pressure curtain rods can be utilized in the same way. They also come in variable lengths, ranging from 36″–60″ to 48″–72″.

As a Freestanding Element

If wall space is limited, build a freestanding pole. However, the caution implicit in this suggestion is that simple hanging from a cord allows the banner to swing or slide back and forth. This problem is solved by adding a rigid horizontal pole to the top of the stand (see illustration).

Procedure

1. All materials for the stand can be found at a building materials supplier. The vertical pole can be wood or metal. It should be at least a foot longer than the banners it is to support and long enough to enable a seated congregation to see the banner.

2. Look in the plumbing supplies for a PVC pipe T-fitting for the top end. It should fit so tightly that gluing is unnecessary. Simply jamb it onto one end of the pole and give it a few taps with a hammer.

3. For the crossbar, buy a wooden dowel the same diameter as the vertical pole, cut the dowel in half and jamb the halves into the openings of the T.

4. For a base, cut two squares of 3/4″ plywood, one 18″ × 18″ and one 12″ × 12″. Stack them and nail or screw them together. Drill a hole in the center of the diameter of the vertical pole.

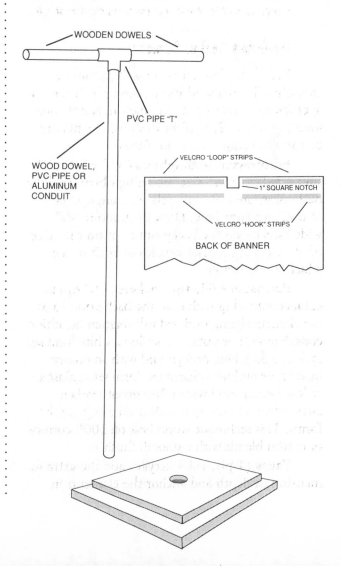

WOODEN DOWELS

PVC PIPE "T"

WOOD DOWEL, PVC PIPE OR ALUMINUM CONDUIT

VELCRO "LOOP" STRIPS

1″ SQUARE NOTCH

VELCRO "HOOK" STRIPS

BACK OF BANNER

5. To prepare the banner for hanging, cut a 1″ square notch in the center of the top edge of the banner. With Velcro adhesive, attach Velcro loop strips to the back of the banner from the sides to the notch along the top edge. Then, attach hook strips 3″ down from and parallel to the top edge. To hang, drape the banner over the top of the horizontal pole and mate the Velcro strips. This method is quite practical, especially for processional banners.

Banners are works of art created for the specific purposes of enhancing worship, encouraging activity, and glorifying God. They should not be seen as merely decorative adornments, to add a note of interest or a splash of color to otherwise drab surroundings. Nor should they be seen as elaborate craft projects. Bannermakers should be confident in their work. There is no need for added gimmicks such as fringe, tassels, or decorative ribbons. Such trims have a place on throw pillows, draperies, and other home projects. But, on banners, especially the designs in this book, they are unnecessary. Not only do they detract from the feeling of the designs, but they also, in practical terms, tend to loosen or unravel, creating a maintenance problem.

Learning Useful Techniques

LETTERING

Letterspacing

Proper spacing of individual letters in a word is vitally important to the overall appearance and readability of a banner. Inconsistent or cramped spacing makes the viewer more conscious of the letters than the words.

If every letter were rectangular, then spacing would be easy. It would merely be a matter of measuring equal distances between rectangles, as with this group:

HMN

But the variety in widths and shapes of individual letters makes this impossible. The only pure rectangles in the modern alphabet are HMN (previous column). Look what happens to this even spacing when curved or irregular forms are introduced:

NHAOCYTI

Everything seems out of place, especially the A and Y. As these examples demonstrate, letter spacing cannot be left to chance. Nor can it be determined by a rigid set of rules. It is done aesthetically, by eye, so that the spaces appear to be even. This is not as difficult as it sounds. The human eye is easily deceived.

Compare these two rectangles. Which is larger?

To most people, the vertical one appears to be larger, but in actuality, both rectangles are the same size.

To space lettering correctly, imagine that the blank areas between letters are filled with water, and try as much as possible to equalize the area the eye must "swim" to read from letter to letter. When lettering is properly spaced, the amount of liquid between letters appears to be the same.

Spaced by eye, the lettering from above appears as follows:

NHAOCYTI

General Lettering Principles

The letters needing the most space between them are those made with single strokes, such as *i* and *l*. They need breathing room to keep from seeming squashed.

illi

Slightly less space is needed between rectangular letters, for instance, *M* and *N*.

MN

A medium space is needed between a rectangular letter and a rounded letter, for instance, *N* and *O*, or *n* and *d*.

NO nd

Even less space is needed between two rounded letters, such as, *O* and *C*, or *b* and *o*.

OC bo

The odd but frequent combinations such as *A* and *T*, *V* and *Y*, or *L* and *T* can be virtually abutted, or even allowed to touch or overlap. Their distinctive shapes make them easy to distinguish.

AT VY LT

With letter spacing, there is actually only one absolute: set rules aside and trust the eye. Beginners usually space the letters too widely, but with practice the spacing will become tighter.

Word Spacing

For banners, a good rule of thumb for determining the spacing of words is to use the width of an *N* as a starting point, keeping in mind that words, like letters, are spaced by eye and not by some arbitrary and regular measurement. It is possible to use narrower spacing if working area is limited, but the words should never be so tightly spaced that they blend into alphabet soup, nor so widely spaced that they lose their flow and readability. The only way to acquire this all important skill is to practice.

Letter Size

The word *Christ* below illustrates another important lettering principle.

Christ
Christ

When guidelines are added, as in the second example, it becomes apparent that the letter forms with curves are relatively larger. This is standard practice for all lettering, both typeset and hand drawn. It is yet another deception necessary to compensate for the perception of the human eye.

For example, compare these two shapes without measuring. Which is taller?

The rectangle appears taller to the eye, but measurement reveals that they are both the same height. Because of the way the eye perceives rounded shapes, letters like *C*, *G*, *J*, and *O* are always made slightly larger. On a banner, this can be 1/4″–1″, sometimes even more, depending on the banner scale. Applying this principle will make the same shapes appear more equal.

Line Spacing

In general, the minimum amount of space between lines of lettering is the amount needed so that the descenders (see Glossary) of the letters in the upper line will not become confused with the ascenders of the letters in the lower line.

All things proclaim the existence of God

Notice how the g in the top line interferes with the t in the bottom line. It is also difficult to read. Below, the same lines are shown properly spaced.

All things proclaim

the existence of God

Capital letters, which have no ascenders or descenders, can be spaced quite closely and still be distinguished.

HE HAS MADE ALL THINGS NEW

A Short Glossary of Lettering Terms

- Ascenders—the parts of lowercase letters extending above the main body, for example, *b, d, h, k.*
- Baseline—the invisible guideline on which a line of lettering sits.
- Descenders—the parts of lowercase letters extending below the main body, for example, *g, j, p, q, y.*
- Lowercase—commonly known as small letters; so called because, in printing, these characters are kept in the lower cases or trays of type cabinets.
- Sans serif—a type style without serifs, for example, Aa Bb Cc Dd Ee Ff Gg Hh Ii
- Serif—the decoration on the end of a letter stroke, for example, Aa Bb Cc Dd Ee Ff Gg Hh Ii
- Uppercase—commonly known as capital letters; so-called because, in printing, these characters are kept in the upper cases or trays of type cabinets.

Lettering is an intricate and fascinating art. Keeping the principles of this section in mind makes it less difficult at first and easy later on.

Quick Lettering Patterns

Custom banners are often commissioned for weddings, anniversaries, or other special occasions where planning and construction time is limited. Most of that valuable time is often spent on patterns for the lettering. It would be easy if it were possible to paint the words directly on the background. But paint and cloth are not that compatible, and it is difficult to achieve a professional look by this method. There are other lettering techniques, however, that do yield professional results with minimal effort.

Hand-Lettering

Materials

- Sheets of newsprint
- Masking tape or glue stick
- 12 oz. can of spray paint (red is a good contrast to the black print on the paper) OR
- A pint can of quick-drying enamel and an inexpensive 1″–1 1/2″ wide natural-bristle brush

Procedure

1. Glue or tape newspaper sheets together into one piece equal in size to the finished banner.

2. In a well-ventilated area (perhaps a garage) tack the paper sheet to the wall at eye level (or lay it on the floor). Keep extra sheets handy to allow for mistakes.

3. *With spray paint*: Hold can 3″–6″ from the paper and write the words in order starting at the upper left. A cursive style with simplified strokes generally works best. After drying, the strokes can be refined with a felt-tip marker.

4. *With enamel and brush*: Use the best possible block lettering style and remember that

mistakes are easily corrected during cutting.

5. Cut letters out and use like any other pattern.

The results of hand-lettering are spontaneous and personal.

Book Lettering

Materials

- A photocopier.
- An X-Acto knife or a pair of sharp scissors.
- A book on calligraphy, typography, or lettering that shows complete alphabets in different styles. (Section 745.6 of the local library should have a choice of such books.)

Procedure

1. Make copies of the desired styles of lettering and add them to the design notebook. Be sure to include all letters and examples of both upper and lowercase letters for each chosen alphabet. Bold styles work best. Look for sans serif typefaces such as: Futura Display, Avant Garde, or Franklin Gothic. Look for serif typefaces such as: Goudy Bold, or Garamond Bold. As an alternative, look for simulated handwriting: Kaufman Script.

2. When lettering is needed for a project, e.g., adding the names of the bride and bridegroom to a wedding banner, it is then easy to choose an appropriate style from among the alphabets already stored in the design notebook.

3. Set the photocopier to maximum enlargement percentage and copy the sample alphabet. Copy these enlargements successively until the letters are scaled to the needed size. It will take several steps, but it is quicker and more accurate than tracing by hand.

4. Carefully cut out the individual letters with an X–Acto knife or sharp scissors.

The results of book lettering will be stylish and consistent.

Computer-Generated Lettering

This technique saves a lot of tracing and increases accessibility to a variety of lettering styles.

Materials

- A computer
- A printer
- A photocopier

Procedure

1. Select the font and size of typeface (probably, as large as possible, depending upon the machine).

2. Type the words needed for the banner and print them out.

3. If necessary, enlarge the letters using the photocopier. Very large sizes may reproduce only one letter per sheet of paper.

Save toner by designating the font as an outline.

Three full-alphabet lettering styles (or fonts as today's computer literate world would call them) are included on pages 20-22. As you page through this book, you will see them used in several designs. You will find them especially helpful when creating your own banner designs, or for personalizing a banner design by adding one or several names (for weddings, confirmations, graduations, etc.).

To utilize a selected style, enlarge the entire page on a photocopier set to its maximum enlargement percentage (156% for many copiers). If all the letters don't fit on a single page, copy them in sections. Copy each successive enlargement until the letters are the size needed for the completed design.

FUTURA

ABCDEFGHIJK
LMNOPQRSTU
VWXYZ&?.,-

abcdefghijklm
nopqrstuvwxyz

ABCDEFGHIJK
LMMNOPQRSTU
VWXYZ&?.,-

abcdefghijklmno
pqurstuvwxyz

FRIZ QUADRATA

ABCDEFGHIJ
KLMNOPQRS
TUVWXYZ&?
.,-abcdefghi
jklmnopqrst
uvwxyz
ABCDEFGHIJK
LMNOPQRSTU
VWXYZ&?.,-
abcdefghijklm
nopqrstuvwxyz

AD LIB

ABCDEFG
HIJKLMN
OPQRSTU
VWXYZ
abcdefghi
jklmnopqr
stuvwxyz
& ?'„'

COMBINING COLORS

Choosing Colors

There are several ways to coordinate colors for a banner.

A color wheel can be useful, but it also carries the danger of turning what could be an artistic process into a merely mechanical one.

Another place to turn for ready-to-go color combinations is a fabric dealer. Pay particular attention to floral prints and other multicolored fabrics. Purchase narrow strips of the best of them. Add them to the design notebook and then borrow three or four colors from one of the swatches when other ideas do not seem to work.

The best place to look is the natural world, where the glories of God's creation appear in infinitely beautiful combinations. Sunrises reveal magentas, purples, peaches, reds, oranges, pinks, blues, and yellows. They give way to a sky filled with shades of blue, gray, and white. From there, turn to the purple and blue mountains, green trees with brown trunks, and flowers combining variegated greens with reds, yellows, oranges, violets, and pinks. Nature provides a color wheel to stir the imagination. Use a camera to capture especially striking color combinations and add them to the design notebook for ready reference.

Special Rainbow Technique

It is possible to create a stunning effect by literally painting the colors into the fabric of a banner. Use this technique, for instance, on the Baptism banner (p. 40) to turn the lettering into a rainbow.

Materials

- Empty 1–2 gallon plastic bucket
- 2 fl. oz. tubes of artist's acrylic paint in red, orange, yellow, green, blue, and violet
- An inexpensive 1"–1 1/2" wide natural-bristle brush
- 2 1/2 yds. 100% cotton flannel, prewashed
- Spray bottle for water
- A large, smooth, flat work area, ideally a concrete floor, or, a sheet of plywood

Procedure

1. Lay cloth on work surface and spray with warm water to dampen evenly.

2. Squeeze about 1/4– 1/3 of the red acrylic paint into the bucket and, with the paint brush, stir while gradually adding about a pint of water; mix thoroughly. Though watery, the diluted color will retain surprising intensity.

3. To avoid unwanted blotches, rinse brush and squeeze dry.

4. Paint a 5"– 6" × 7' red stripe along one edge of the cloth, making sure the color is evenly spread.

5. Empty and rinse bucket.

6. Repeat steps 2 through 5 with, in succession, orange, yellow, green, blue, and violet. Slightly overlap the bands of color so they will blend naturally into each other. The six colored stripes should cover a 34"–36" wide area.

7. *Allow to dry flat.* Do not hang up in an attempt to lessen drying time. Gravity will pull color pigments downward, creating a muddy mess near the bottom.

8. Once thoroughly dry, the rainbow fabric can be treated like any other cloth. Lay it *face* side up on a flat surface. Arrange letter patterns *right* side up on top. It is important that they be aligned properly so the rainbow effect does not appear jumbled on the completed banner. Trace with a No. 2 pencil or a colored pencil.

9. If bonding with glue: cut out the letters, position carefully and follow the gluing procedure in "Putting the Banner Together."

10. If bonding with an iron-on adhesive: fuse adhesive sheets to the back of the painted fabric and cut out the letters. *Test with scraps cut from the edges to be sure the paint does not interfere with the bonding process.* If satisfied with the results, proceed as directed in "Putting the Banner Together."

11. Any time an iron is used on this fabric, use a damp pressing cloth to protect the fabric. Otherwise the paint will scorch or leave a residue on the sole plate of the iron.

Somewhat the same effect can be achieved with 6" wide strips of cloth, one in each of the six colors. Use 1/2" wide strips of fusible web to bond them together into a single piece. (Either method will create an eye-catching effect, but, while somewhat messy, the painting technique is more spontaneous and personal.)

AN EXERCISE IN CREATIVITY

The main purpose of this exercise is to utilize the odd fabric scraps accumulated from other projects.

Materials

- Background fabric, preferably felt
- Fusible web, sufficient to cover background
- Boxes of saved fabric scraps
- Sharp scissors
- Assorted items necessary for finishing and hanging (pins, lining material, Stitch Witchery, etc.)

Procedure

1. Pick a size for the banner—2′ × 8′ or 3′ × 6′ are good proportions—and purchase background material in either dark blue or dark green (these colors provide a good contrast to most other colors).

2. Cut background to size, adding necessary hem and casing allowances. Place *face side up* on the work surface.

3. Pick a word theme. One of joy or praise is best. One that comes immediately to mind is *Let all creation sing.* The Psalms are a good place to go for inspiration, for example, "Sing to the LORD" (Psalm 147:7), or, "I will praise the LORD all my life" (Psalm 146:2). Lines from favorite hymns are also excellent, for example, "Lift every voice and sing."

4. For the lettering, use patterns saved from other projects from which to randomly select the letters needed (it does not matter if they are not the same style). Arrange them on the background to see how they work together. Or experiment with the quick lettering techniques described earlier.

5. Pick through the fabric scrap collection to find pieces and colors that stand out against the background.

6. Put fusible adhesive *paper side up* on a flat surface. Reverse the letter patterns and trace them with a pencil. Space them closely to minimize waste.

7. Cut out the letters and fuse them to the back of the fabric scraps. Let them cool, cut around the fused letters, and peel off the paper backing. Arrange the letters on the background material in a tightly spaced block roughly covering the upper two-thirds of the banner.

8. On the remainder of the adhesive sheet, sketch imaginative shapes inspired by nature (flowers, birds, trees, human figures, stars, wavy lines for water, swirls for clouds). Keep them simple and childlike. (This would be a good project for a Sunday school class.)

9. Cut out the shapes and, as with the letters, fuse them to the back of the randomly selected scraps. Let them cool, cut them out, and peel off the paper backing.

10. Position the shapes *adhesive side down,* around the block of lettering (See item 7). Readjust until a pleasing arrangement is achieved. Fuse everything in place as described earlier.

11. To finish, attach the lining and secure hems and casings as needed.

Free-form banners such as this one are not only a joy to produce, but they also often generate favorable responses. They work well during the long after-Pentecost summer months when variety is pleasant.

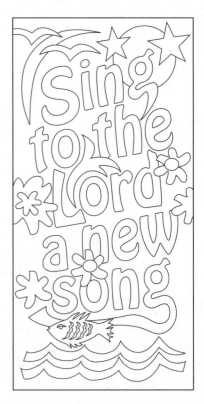

SELF-DESIGN

Brainstorming Method

The best way to get creative juices flowing and thus come up with a great idea for a banner design is to utilize the process of brainstorming, otherwise known as thumbnailing. With notebook or sketch pad in hand, quickly sketch out lots of ideas as fast as possible no matter how radical or improbable. Remember, nothing is more limiting than *one* idea. Thumbnails, as the term implies, should be small (about 2″) so they all fit on one or two pages. When there are at least 10 ideas, sift them and begin eliminating ideas until only 2 or 3 are left. Enlarge and polish these, refining graphic forms and lines and sorting through possible colors. Next, pick the best one of these, turn it into a line drawing (like the ones in this book), and copy it onto an overhead projection transparency. It is now possible to transform that idea into a physical reality.

A key component of the creative process is flexibility. The mind needs to be kept open to possibilities. As work proceeds, continue to question, explore, and adapt. Would an element work better in a different color? Would a rough or smooth texture accent a particular area? Does the addition of this shape upset the overall design? Is the slogan too long? These are just a few of the questions that might be asked and, if the answer to any is yes, acted upon.

Spontaneous Method

Another, more immediate, way to create a design is to use the spontaneous approach.

Materials

- Background cloth (felt is a good choice because it does not require lining) in a favorite color, and in a size and proportion to fit the display area. Make necessary hem allowances for hanging.

- 1/2 yd. each of three or four different colors of a mostly cotton fabric for the design pieces (try broadcloth or poly-cotton sheeting). Coordinate these colors with each other and the background, being sure they work together well.

- Fusible web, for bonding. Purchase enough material to totally cover the cloth for the design pieces.

- Sharp scissors.

- Iron and pressing cloth

Procedure

1. Place the background on the floor so it can be looked at from a distance and from different perspectives.

2. Bond the fusible adhesive to the back of the fabric for the design elements, following the directions furnished with the material.

3. If the word theme has not been chosen, open the Bible to the Psalms, or a hymnal anywhere, and begin reading through the verses or stanzas and, without analyzing them, jotting down any phrases that strike a responsive chord. Do not stop with one.

4. Begin sifting through the choices, tossing out the inappropriate ones or even rewriting them until there is one phrase left that suits the banner. With a large marker, write it down as a reminder while work proceeds.

5. With scissors in hand, begin cutting out the letters. Use a variety of colors or just one. Try cutting directly without relying on pencil guidelines. When finished, peel off the paper backing and place it loosely on the background *cloth side up.* This will give a good idea of how much space there is to work with.

6. Next, cut out a variety of silhouette shapes in different colors. They can be geometric (squares, circles, triangles), linear (curves, zig-zags, straight orthogonals), organic (animals, heavenly bodies, plants). Let the chosen phrase suggest ideas. Try not to use predrawn guidelines. This may seem difficult at first, but it is possible to *feel* the shapes and actually draw with the scissors. As the shapes are cut, peel off the paper backing and place them on the background with the letters. Often just the process of doing a preliminary arrangement will suggest possibilities for other shapes.

7. Spaces are either positive or negative. Positive space is the shape itself. Negative space is the empty area around the shape, and it is as important to any design as the positive space. Keep this in mind as you move the shapes and

letters around the background, looking for a pleasing arrangement. Not all the negative space needs to be filled. Watch the negative spaces change as the shapes are moved to new positions. Also, instead of lumping the lines of letters into a single block, split them and work the shapes in between or turn them vertically or at an angle. This is the time to learn and experiment, because nothing is fastened permanently. For a change of perspective, stand up, walk around, and look at everything from the top or sides.

8. Finalize the arrangement. Be sure the letters are properly spaced. Preheat the iron. Follow the instructions with the fusible web for bonding. Add hems to the top and bottom and hang.

Finding a Niche

No matter how a banner is conceived and finally executed, it is important always to keep its ultimate purpose in mind. Banners are designed to play an important part in worship, and they do that best when they are well placed.

Banners are frequently displayed in the vicinity of the altar, table, or podium. But not all worship-related activities take place directly to the front. When worshippers turn to observe the choir, are their eyes confronted by an expanse of blank wall? As guests and members leave a meaningful worship experience, does the narthex or hallway outside the sanctuary serve only as egress to the parking lot? These are only two of the areas that bannermakers can utilize to subtly extend the worship experience or to invite people to participate in other church activities.

Remember, banners are not sales tools, like newspaper ads, nor are they propaganda, like posters. They are meant to excite, provoke thought, and create an atmosphere conducive to worship. Part of what makes banners interesting is that once they are put on display, they take on a life of their own. People not only see them, they experience them, and, depending upon their personal outlooks, draw different things from them.

A Word on Color

Early in the Bible, color was connected with meaningful worship. Beginning in Ex. 26:1,

God, through Moses, instructs the Israelites to "make the tabernacle with ten curtains of finely twisted linen and blue, purple and scarlet yarn . . . "

The early church apparently used white throughout the year. Color to differentiate the seasons appeared gradually between the 9th and 13th centuries. It was not until the 16th century, however, that the church established the now familiar sequence of red, green, violet, black, and white. By virtue of their inherent moods and characteristics, these colors have subtly influenced worship for many decades.

Red (5), for example, is the warm color of life-giving blood. It is passion, love, caring, and sentimentality, but it can also be anger, sublimation, and war. Of all the colors of worship, it is the most powerful. A large splash of red demands attention. In liturgy, the church reserves red to commemorate Pentecost, Reformation, Palm Sunday, ordinations, and the days of various saints. These festivals, representing high emotion and God's call to action, like the color, cannot be ignored.

Green (14), the church's non-festival color, designates the two transitional periods known on the church calendar as "after the Epiphany" and "after Pentecost." Labeling them as such seems to imply that these periods are routine and unexciting. It is rather better to think of them as times of learning and growth in faith, times that challenge artists to find different and exciting ways to lend visual emphasis to the rich variety of messages from Jesus' ministry. Here, the vibrancy of the greens chosen is very important. These seasons call for the deep natural shades of summer leaves and grass.

The western world associates **black (2)** with mourning, absence, darkness, and death. Therefore, the church uses it only once, for the day of supreme seriousness, Good Friday. For bannermakers, however, it is an excellent background color. Virtually all other colors seem to advance, to pop out, when placed against it. Use black with restraint, because, as such a strong color, its effect can be overwhelming.

White (1) is the festival color of the church. In liturgy, it is reserved for celebrations that reflect themes of purity, light, innocence, holiness, and redemption, including Jesus' birth, baptism, transfiguration, and resurrection; Maundy Thursday and Thanksgiving. For the banner-maker it presents challenges. Although it is easy to use for letters and other design elements, as a background it can be intimidating. It tends to dominate, forcing boldness in the choice of colors and graphics. Timidity in the presence of white only results in design elements that get lost.

Violet (20) is most often associated with the Lenten season. As a combination of warm red (passion) and cool blue (calm), neither moving nor still, violet perfectly represents this most necessary season that refocuses from Jesus' hopeful birth to his agonizing death. Violet is preferable to purple for Lent, because purple suggests the pagan Roman imperium. Violet gives a truer portrayal of Lent's themes of humility, penitence, sorrow, and grief.

Blue (19) best represents the other season of thoughtful preparation, Advent. It gives Advent its own identity. In a worship setting, blue creates an atmosphere akin to that of darkness becoming light, of a new day dawning, filled with possibilities. And, like black, it is very accommodating; it works well with virtually any color. There is no better color to signify the beginning of the church year.

The nonliturgical color **yellow (11)** endows the worship environment with the glow and warmth of the sun. Used for Easter, it generates thoughts of the enlightening revelation of Jesus' empty tomb that vanquishes death and despair forever.

Throughout the church year, the varying colors used in worship unfold as a rainbow, affirming the constant presence of God's grace in the life of the individual Christian. Like Joseph's many-colored coat, the colors signify the believer as God's firstborn and heir to his promise of eternal life.

The Church Year

Advent Rose Series
Is. 11:1, Is. 35:1

In the Holy Land the winter rains combine with the warmth of spring to produce a colorful array of blossoms. Arid desert areas burst into a showy display that lasts until the summer droughts again dry up the landscape. Old Testament writers such as Isaiah saw in this imagery a metaphor for the coming of the Messianic age: "The desert and the parched land will be glad; the wilderness will rejoice and blossom" (Is. 35:1).

One of the greatest romantic images of Advent is the wild rose blooming in the desert, heralding Jesus' birth in fulfillment of the prophecies (see Is. 11:1). This opening series of designs gives life to that imagery. It comprises four separate designs placed back-to-back on two banners. Display a different side each week so that the rose appears to "grow" as Advent advances toward Christmas.

It is possible to give depth and an added sense of realism to the flowers by using washable markers to shade the flower petals. See the description of the procedure with the Epiphany banner on page 32.

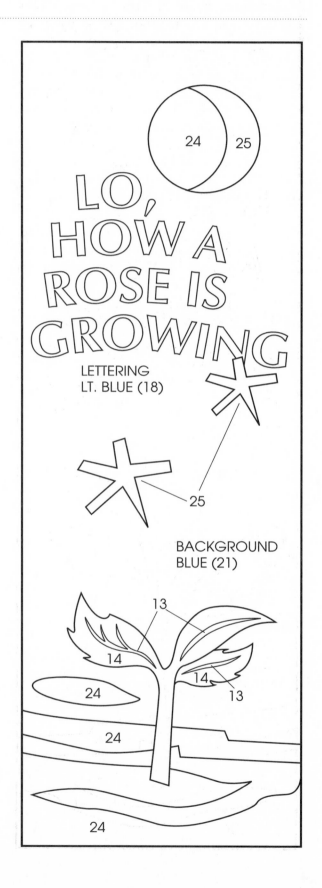

BACKGROUND
BLUE (21)

24

25

24

LETTERING
LT. BLUE (18)

AS THE
PROPHETS
FORETOLD

24

13

7

13

14

24

24

24

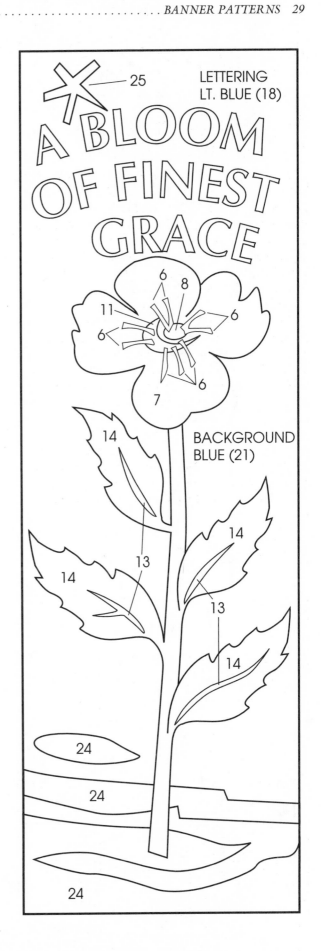

25

LETTERING
LT. BLUE (18)

A BLOOM
OF FINEST
GRACE

6   8
11   6
6
6
7

14

13

14

13

14

BACKGROUND
BLUE (21)

14

13

24

24

24

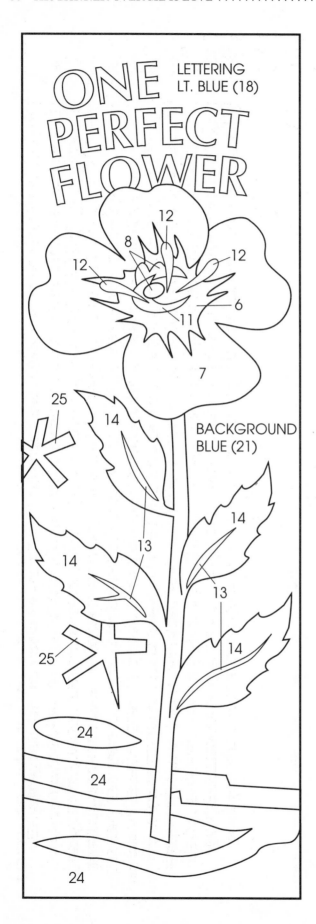

Christmas Star
Num. 24:17

This design, with its added dimension of depth, defies the traditional definition of "banner." You will be making what is essentially a large pillow. The star, a symbol of victory, will help point the way to the Christ child during your Christmas celebrations. (Construction of the Pentecost dove, a reminder of the manifestation of the Holy Spirit at Pentecost that gave birth to the church, follows the same bias procedure. Exceptions are given at the end.)

Materials

- Two pieces of heavy white cloth, 30″ × 30″ (felt, poplin, for example)
- 4 or 5, 20 oz. bags polyester fiberfill for stuffing
- Sewing needle and heavy duty white thread
- Straight pins
- Fishing line, 25 lb. test or heavier for hanging

Procedure

1. Follow the "No-Pattern Method" to enlarge the star/dove (see p. 10). Make two pieces. Cut them out and place on work surface, aligning them to each other. (The optional decorative shapes should be bonded to one of the halves at this point. See below.)

2. Set sewing machine to "straight stretch stitch." Pin pieces together along edges and sew edges together with ⅝″ seam, leaving a 6″ opening, as indicated, for stuffing.

3. Reach through opening and turn inside out, as with a pillow case.

4. Beginning with points, stuff tightly (to prevent sagging after hanging) with polyester fiber fill. Close opening by hand with needle and thread.

5. As indicated, attach streamers to back with needle and thread.

6. Thread large sewing needle with a double strand of fishing line (for added security). Attach fishing line to the back of the star/dove at a point about 3″ above center.

7. Decide on a place in the sanctuary for display. It will look best suspended from the ceiling or a support beam, away from the wall. Place screw eye at that point and hang star/dove at an appro-

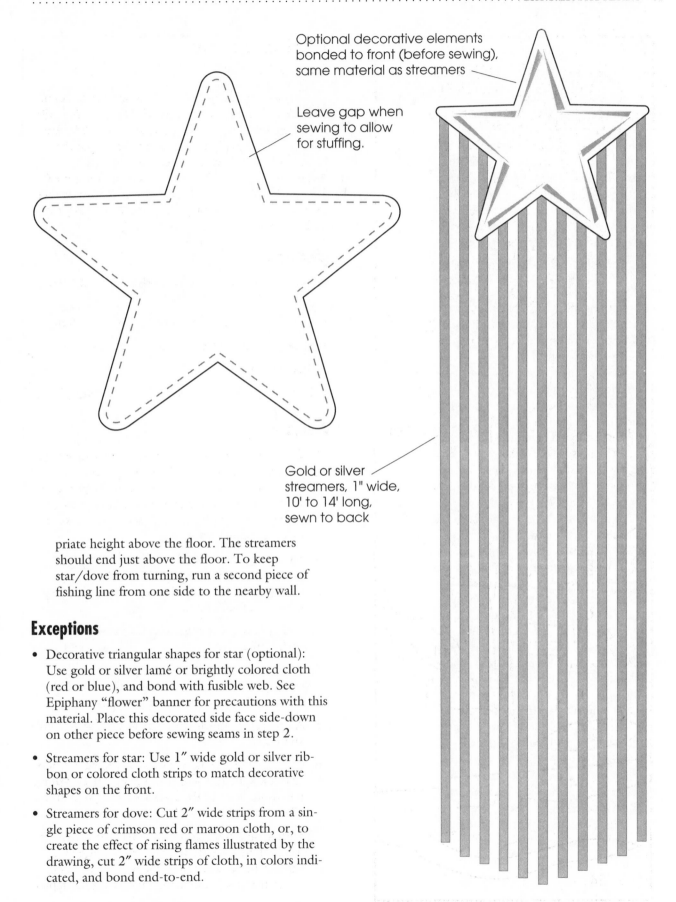

Optional decorative elements bonded to front (before sewing), same material as streamers

Leave gap when sewing to allow for stuffing.

Gold or silver streamers, 1" wide, 10' to 14' long, sewn to back

priate height above the floor. The streamers should end just above the floor. To keep star/dove from turning, run a second piece of fishing line from one side to the nearby wall.

Exceptions

- Decorative triangular shapes for star (optional): Use gold or silver lamé or brightly colored cloth (red or blue), and bond with fusible web. See Epiphany "flower" banner for precautions with this material. Place this decorated side face side-down on other piece before sewing seams in step 2.

- Streamers for star: Use 1″ wide gold or silver ribbon or colored cloth strips to match decorative shapes on the front.

- Streamers for dove: Cut 2″ wide strips from a single piece of crimson red or maroon cloth, or, to create the effect of rising flames illustrated by the drawing, cut 2″ wide strips of cloth, in colors indicated, and bond end-to-end.

Epiphany
Is. 60:1

Epiphany celebrates the manifestation of Christ to the Magi and the whole world. The symbols associated with the story in Matthew's gospel—the star, the Wise Men and their gifts of gold, frankincense, and myrrh—offer many possibilities for artistic expression. They have become a bit shopworn. A little research provides a different angle for artistic expression, based on the sources of gold, frankincense, and myrrh.

In biblical times frankincense was used for secular purposes as a perfume and in religious rituals as incense. It comes from the excretions of the boswellia tree that grows in Arabia, Ethiopia, and India. Its starlike flower, recalls the star that guided the Magi to the infant Jesus.

Myrrh is an aromatic resin derived from various shrubs and trees, including the rockrose found primarily in Arabia and India. Highly prized in ancient times as both an incense and a perfume, myrrh adds a note of irony to the Epiphany story because it was possibly one of the spices the three women bought to anoint Jesus' body in the tomb (Mark 16:1).

To represent the gift of gold, use gold lamé in the background areas indicated with a "G." Choose a solid, not variegated, shade. Caution: Lamé is thin and unravels easily. Both problems can be fixed by using a fusible web for bonding especially made for lightweight fabrics. It prevents the adhesive from seeping through onto the surface of this rather filmy and porous material. Also, lamé is heat sensitive. Care should be taken not to place a hot iron directly on it. Always cover it with a damp pressing cloth when ironing it. If any adhesive migrates onto the front surface, it can be gently scratched off with your fingernails.

To give added depth to the flowers, use washable marking pens to shade the flower petals (see the shaded areas in the design). Then, with an inexpensive watercolor brush, dampen the area with tap water. The marker will bleed creating a subtle shaded area.

BACKGROUND
GRAY (3)

Lent

No other event in the life of Christ has been represented in art more than the crucifixion. Early Christians avoided showing Christ suspended on the cross. Such depictions are not found until the mid fourth century, and most show him still alive, reflecting a focus on the resurrection. After the Black Death in 1348 Europeans seemed preoccupied with death. The crucifixes of that time reflected this, especially in Germany and Spain, where they bordered on the macabre. This crucifix banner, like the crucifixes of the early church, shows Christ, not in the throes of death (there is no cross), but as a conquering hero with his arms raised in victory, reaching outward to claim us with his all-encompassing love.

There is nothing timid about this design. It is meant to startle and grab attention. Don't allow the possible reaction of others to deter you from trying this design. Some might find it unsettling, even shocking, but surely no more so than the crucifixion itself, where a human life, stretched out for all to see, struggled against the pressure of his own body weight to maintain breathing over a period of many hours, even days. This banner may bring home the Gospel message of Christ's saving act in a way no words can express.

The background should be a deep violet, the color of Lent. For the figure of Christ use bright crimson red, a reminder of his struggle to win the final victory. The design can be completed totally with cloth, using the instructions given in the opening pages. However, the most stunning and visually stimulating effect is achieved with paint.

ALL PARTS OF FIGURE
CRIMSON RED (5)

BACKGROUND
VIOLET (23)

Materials

- 2 1/2 yds. (approx.) of 100% natural cotton muslin

- Inexpensive 2″ natural bristle brush

- 1 qt. crimson red latex paint, or a 2 fl. oz. tube of bright red artist's acrylic paint

- 1 gal. container for mixing paint

- #2 pencils, or Prismacolor pencils

- Masking tape

- Sharp scissors

- Dark violet cloth for the background, preferably felt

- White craft glue for bonding with less porous materials

Procedure

1. Decide on a final size for the figure of Christ, life size, about 6′ high, is most effective.

2. Copy the figure onto a projection transparency.

3. Project the design directly onto a wall.

4. Use a 12′ tape measure to size the image to the size of the finished banner.

5. Attach the piece of cloth to the wall over the image area with masking tape.

6. Trace all the shapes making up the figure of Christ onto the cloth with a pencil.

7. Lay the cloth on a flat work surface. Thin the paint with about 1 cup water. Paint all the shapes that comprise the figure of Christ, working quickly to retain spontaneity. There is no need to be too careful. The whole process should take 15–20 minutes. Allow to dry thoroughly before handling.

8. Before cutting out the Christ figure from the muslin, arrange the muslin on the violet background cloth, in final position. This will eliminate time-consuming reassembly during the bonding process.

9. Carefully cut around the paint strokes, while attempting to maintain their rough, spontaneous quality. Keep in mind that when the banner is finished, the figure of Christ should look as if it were painted directly on the background.

10. Bond the cut-out pieces to the violet background with the white craft glue. (See "Gluing Method," p. 11.) When completed, step away and survey your work.

Easter

Whereas Christmas is a quiet, contemplative celebration, filled with feelings of warmth, peace, and quiet joy, Easter is an unabashed, no-holds-barred party. Alleluias, set aside during the six weeks of Lent, return in a big way "Christ is risen … He is risen indeed! Alleluia!" This design features a bold Alleluia to get the party rolling.

Although white is designated for the background, a bold, bright yellow would work equally well.

The Holy Trinity
We All Believe in One True God

The Holy Trinity traditionally is represented by symbols such as three linked rings or an equilateral triangle combined with a circle. These symbols evolved at a time when society was largely illiterate, and served as "books" to help uneducated people understand a difficult concept about God.

Liturgical artists continue to search for new ways to express timeless truths. Traditional Trinity symbols signify that our God is both "triune" (Father, Son, Spirit) and eternal, without beginning or end. But they tell us nothing about the interaction of the three persons with our lives.

The initial inspiration for this design came from several Trinity hymns, including "We All Believe in One True God." Descriptive action words were noted while reading through these stanzas from which three were chosen that best describe the actions of each person of the Trinity. These words are arranged with no space between, thereby leading the eye in a natural flow from one to another, creating a sense of total unity.

BACKGROUND - FOREST GREEN (16)

CREATE REDEEM INSPIRE

LETTERING - WHITE (1)

Pentecost

Cut two pieces white felt 30'
wide. Pin together along edges,
and sew as indicated by dashed
line. As with star, leave gap for
stuffing.

Cut 7 strips burgundy (4)
felt, 1 1/2" to 2" wide X 12'
to 14' long. Bond other
colors to them as indicated.
Then attach to back of
dove with needle and
thread.

Construction of the Pentecost dove, a reminder
of the manifestation of the Holy Spirit at Pentecost,
follows the same procedure used for the Christmas
star. See page 30.

After Pentecost 1
Song of Songs 1:4

Just as the Holy of Holies designates the most sacred part of the Old Testament temple, so Song of Songs refers to a book of superlative poetry. Like any piece of great art, Song of Songs should not be over-analyzed, but rather received as a gift to enjoy. As it is allowed to speak for itself, God's Spirit will work through it.

This design is an example of pure creativity utilizing a trial and error process. Except for the choice of words, it was not preplanned, not even a thumb nail. The lettering came first, then the pair of lines labeled "12." These formed the foundation for everything else. With the addition of each shape and line came the question "What would work best with the other pieces?" Each piece was tried in various places until it "felt right." This proves a good method when creative juices are at an ebb.

After Pentecost 2
Song of Songs 2:11

The changing seasons can affect our moods. Summer's growth, warmth, and life bring a feeling of well-being. Fall offers a fantastic but brief display of color to stimulate the senses. Winter is sometimes associated with depression. Spring lifts a weight from our shoulders. Chapter 2 of the Song of Songs celebrates the arrival of spring. "See! The winter is past; the rains are over and gone. Flowers appear on the earth; the season of singing has come." This banner celebrates with the author.

After Pentecost 3

This design has no specific Scriptural basis. I can only attribute it to the inspiration of the Holy Spirit. I recall writing down these words one Sunday morning upon arriving at church. While driving, I had been listening to the normal Sunday morning pipe organ program on one of our classical radio stations and was particularly struck by the versatility and tremendous range of an 84-rank instrument in Dallas. At that time the words literally popped into my head. While this banner is very appropriate for the Pentecost season, you can also make it work for Christmas or Epiphany by substituting a star for the circle of the sun (see the star above the design).

The Christian Life

Baptism

Every Baptism reminds us that we have been reborn to a new life in Christ. Even when not in use, the baptismal font silently announces the promise of eternal life (Mark 16:16; 1 Peter 3:21). Banners can effectively emphasize the importance of Baptism, whether hung on a wall behind the font or suspended on a pole nearby.

The fish in this design is adapted from one found in the Catacombs, the burial chambers underneath ancient Rome where the Christians gathered in secret to worship. Among the oldest of Christian symbols, the fish reputedly was a secret identification sign during the years when the Roman government aggressively persecuted Christians. The fish remains important in contemporary iconography.

At some point (no one knows when) the figure of the fish was recognized as a sign for the Christ. It is commonly understood to be an acrostic of the first letters of the words in the phrase Jesus (I) Christ (CH), God's (TH) Son (Y), Savior (S), or ICTHYS, the Greek word for "fish." Today, the fish is seen on car bumpers and lapel pins and in advertising, as a testimony of faith and a reminder to Christians everywhere that we have been reborn to a new life in Christ.

Before making this banner, decide if the lettering block is to be a solid color or turned into a rainbow using the special technique described on page 23.

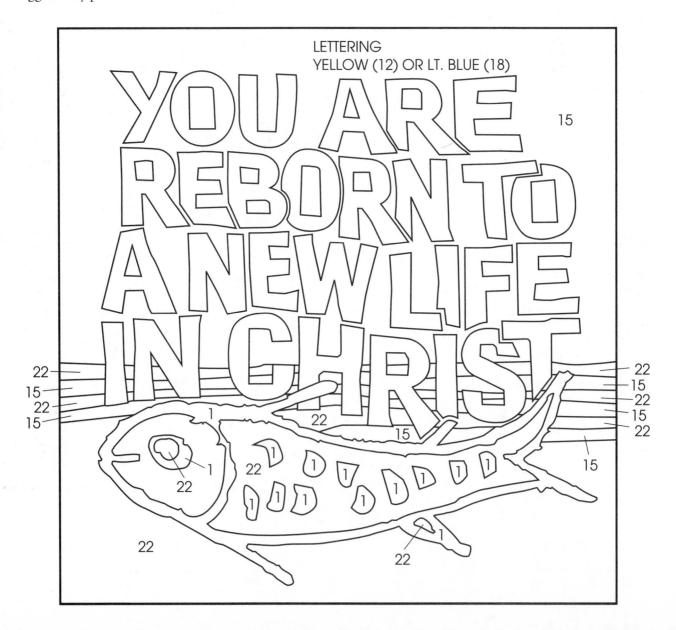

To remember individual Baptisms in a special way, hang streamers along the bottom edge of the banner, with the individual's name on it.

Procedure

1. Prepare a strip of felt 2 1/2″ wide × 18″ long.

2. Photocopy the AD LIB lettering style at the front of this book, enlarging it to 150%. Cut out the letters for the individual's name, reverse them, and trace each letter onto a 3″ wide strip of paper-backed fusible adhesive.

3. With a hot iron fuse the adhesive strip onto a scrap of white cotton broad cloth or similar material.

4. Cut out the letters and remove the paper backing. Position them in one line in the center of the felt strip, and bond them in place.

5. Attach the name strip to the back of the main banner, at the bottom edge, with a safety pin.

6. Throughout the year, add a name for each newly baptized person as a form of an ongoing baptismal roster.

The Lord's Supper

Holy Communion is a feast and a celebration in remembrance of Jesus and his great gift of salvation. This banner design portrays an idyllic communion experience, with everything flowing in perfect harmony, like a well choreographed ballet of worshipers moving forward to receive the bread/body and wine/blood of Christ. The palm branch symbolizes victory through the body and blood of Christ. The circles, floating upwards like balloons, represent the communion elements: the host (light brown) and the wine (violet).

Marriage

The traditional wedding symbol is a Latin cross with two linked rings, symbolizing unity in Christ. This design gives the traditional symbol a contemporary twist. The colors and words are only suggestions. You can easily adapt this design for individual weddings by inviting the bride and groom to choose their own colors or different words, taken either from the Bible or a favorite hymn or saying.

Another possibility is simply to include the names of the couple; e.g., Mary & John. For lettering patterns, see the samples in this book (pp. 20-22), particularly Friz Quadrata. Use one color for both names (preferably, the color of the cross) or use a different color for each; e.g., "John" in teal, "Mary" in blue, and the "&" in fuchsia. Remember that three colors, not including the background, must be selected.

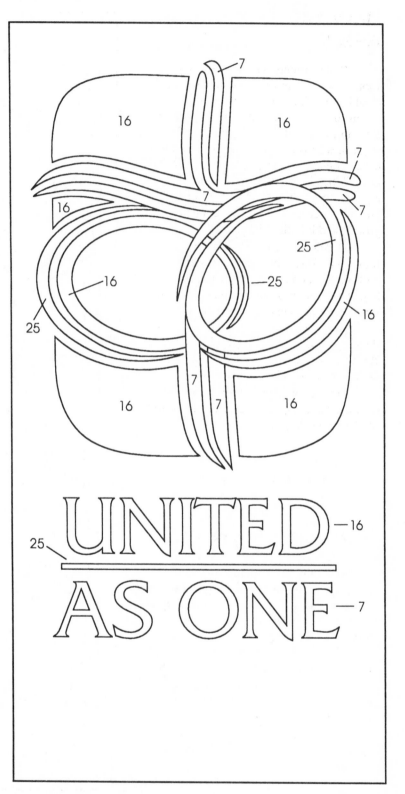

Death

Is. 40:31

While banners seldom are thought about when planning a funeral, a special funeral banner, if already on hand, can be a means of comfort and of Christian witness. Keep in mind that funerals and memorial services, with their special music, floral tributes, Scripture readings, and messages, do not aid the dead. Rather, they offer the living the opportunity to give thanks for the life of the deceased, facilitating the grief process and building faith.

This design, a literal transcription of a thumbnail sketch, began as a small (2″), scribble-like pencil drawing that was enlarged 400% with a photocopier. The lines were then traced exactly to retain the free-form spontaneity and grace of the original sketch. The lettering style, while similar in character to the other lines in the design, nevertheless provides a slight contrast.

This banner is also appropriate for commencements, confirmations, and during the Pentecost season.

Six Lenten Crosses

This series brings us to Golgotha, The Place of the Skull, to confront Jesus' cross and gain an understanding of its meanings for our lives. The series includes several basic and historic cross forms, one for each week in Lent, up to but not including Holy Week, which is usually regarded as separate from Lent.

The cross, among the world's oldest symbols, was used throughout ancient times with many meanings. Countless forms predating the Christian era have been discovered etched or painted on cave walls, pottery pieces, and clay tablets. For example, a form now called the Greek cross with equal-length arms was found among Neanderthal remains carefully inscribed on a round, flat stone. Burial remains in caves in the French Pyrenees have yielded numerous stones painted with red Latin crosses which, archaeologists theorize, depicted the human form with outstretched arms. They are thought to be a burial cult's representation of the souls of the dead. For many cultures the cross portrayed the four cardinal directions, a symbol of totality pointing to all parts of the cosmos. Others saw it as a sun symbol, and still others, particularly the Maya of Central America, saw it as a tree of life providing a link between the heavenly and underground realms.

Early Christians naturally held the cross in high esteem. But, in an era when crucifixions remained a horrible and not uncommon reality, when even the name "Christian" was a vulgar taunt, the open display of a cross—above a small altar in the home or worn on a thong about the neck—invited unwanted attention and ridicule. For example, a crude graffiti scratched on a wall among the ruins of the Palatine in Rome, dating to about AD 200, shows a man with his arms seemingly raised in homage to another man, who had the head of an ass, hanging on a cross. The inscription accompanying this graffiti reads: "Alexomenos worships his god." According to church fathers, early Christians commemorated Christ's saving act with a simple gesture. They made the sign of the cross."

Today, Christians the world over look to the cross as the supreme symbol of Jesus, self-sacrifice in love for the salvation of the world. It is seen everywhere—above altars, carved on the ends of pews, embroidered on vestments, embossed in Bible covers, and hanging on chains about people's necks. Banner designers have a great variety of forms of the cross from which to choose. Foremost among them are those styles believed to have been used in crucifixions: the so-called Latin, St. Andrew's and Tau forms. Then there are the allegorical forms coming from the church's underground period during the time of the great persecutions: the anchor and Chi-Rho. Finally, there are the myriad forms developed during the Middle Ages (in excess of 250, by one accounting) that resulted primarily from the use of the cross as a design element in the coats-of-arms of those knights and others who wished to be remembered for their service in the Crusades.

Cross of Ashes
Matt. 16:24, Luke 9:23

At Baptism when people are joined to Christ's death and rising, they are marked with the cross of Christ. On Ash Wednesday many are again marked with the sign of the cross, this time of ashes, as a reminder of our mortality. It reminds us too that the cross of Jesus was once a tree growing in a forest, which, in turn, recalls the Tree of Life in the garden of Eden. The cross of ashes links us to the cross of Christ and to his call to take up the cross and follow him.

St. Andrew's Cross
Lent 1/John 12:23

When faced with the reality of being the single sacrifice and sin-offering in payment for the sins of the world, Jesus cried to his heavenly Father for relief. But he couldn't avoid God's demand. The hour had come for him to die.

This design features the St. Andrew's Cross, so named because, according to legend, Andrew, the brother of Simon Peter, was executed on a cross in the shape of an × because he felt unworthy of dying on the same cross as his Savior. Aside from its legendary connection, the ×-form is rich in symbolism. The "×" is the Greek letter for "Ch" in English and is a monogram for Christos (Christ). In Roman numerals the "×" represents the value "ten," and ten, as the sum of 1, 2, 3 and 4, is itself symbolic of unity and totality.

The Nail Cross

Lent 2/Creator Spirit, by Whose Aid

"From sin and sorrow set us free," we cry at the foot of the cross as we watch Jesus' painful writhings, as he attempts to raise himself momentarily to relieve the pressure on his lungs to continue breathing. Three nails, one through each arm, and the third through both ankles, hold him securely in place. The three nails in a cruciform shape graphically remind us of Jesus' ordeal.

LETTERING
GRAY (3)

BACKGROUND
WHITE (1)
OR VIOLET (23)

The Latin Cross
Lent 3

The Latin Cross in this design further reminds us of Christ's Good Friday ordeal. Tradition holds that Christ was crucified on a Latin cross, despite the fact that none of the passion narratives include a physical description of the crosses on Golgotha. The primary basis for this long-standing belief is Matt. 27:37, "Above his head they placed the written charge against him: This is Jesus, the king of the Jews." Of the three styles of crosses traditionally used in crucifixions—Tau (T), Latin (†), and St. Andrew's (×)—only the Latin Cross has a vertical arm extending above the horizontal beam where an inscription could be placed.

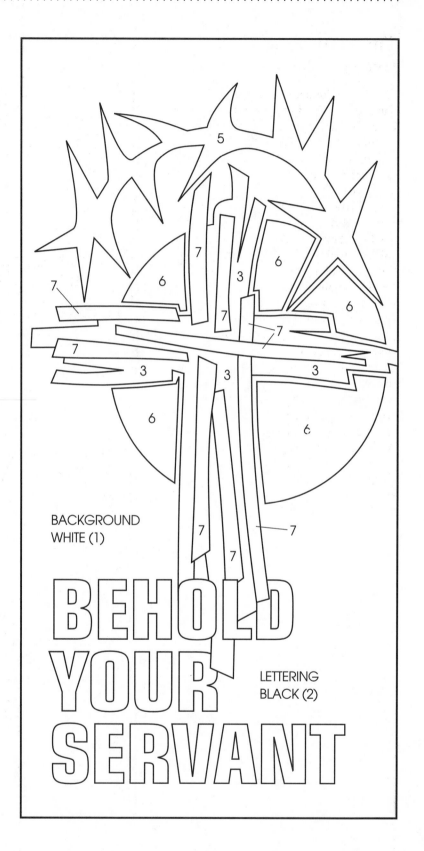

The Jerusalem Cross
Lent 4/John 15:13

The Jerusalem Cross is actually four Tau crosses joined at their bases, with four Greek crosses added between the arms. Historically, it was chosen as the personal coat-of-arms of Godfrey de Boullion, first ruler of the Kingdom of Jerusalem following the city's conquest by the First Crusade in 1099. According to tradition, Godfrey saw this cross during his arduous journey from France to the Holy Land. It is also the symbol of the kingdom of God. With such a long history the Jerusalem Cross naturally acquired several meanings. One source states that the four Greek crosses represent the gospels which supplanted the Old Testament Mosaic Law (represented by the four Tau crosses). The Tau Cross, incidentally, is also known as the Old Testament Cross from its resemblance to the Ankh, the ancient Egyptian symbol of life. As such, it recalls the Israelites' sojourn in Egypt and the Exodus. Another source designates it the five-fold cross, representing the five wounds of Christ (both hands, both feet, and his side cut by the soldier's spear).

The Celtic Cross
Lent 5

The Celtic Cross (also known as the Irish Cross) has oar-shaped arms whose junction is enclosed by a circle. Numerous examples, carved in stone, are found throughout Ireland. They reflect centuries of Irish Christianity that began early in the Christian era, around the fourth century. The Celtic Cross's distinctive shape and rich carved ornamentation make it truly unique. Some Celtic Crosses feature elaborate line and spiral patterns which, like the rings around their junction, symbolize the eternal nature of God. The rings also serve to strengthen the relatively weak junction point. Sometimes Celtic crosses are carved with reliefs depicting familiar biblical stories of God's deliverance: Noah and the ark, Adam and Eve in the garden of Eden, the sacrifice of Isaac, Daniel in the lion's den, and the Baptism of Jesus. Others contain depictions of the 12 disciples and the crucifixion. Of all crossforms, the Celtic Cross is a true reflection of the glory of God.

This design is especially appropriate as a theme banner when focusing on evangelization. The Irish were responsible for carrying the Gospel message to Europe at a time when others had lost their evangelical zeal.

The Psalms

Ps. 4:7
Transfiguration

This series of banner designs is based entirely on psalms. Where appropriate, suggestions for specific uses for banners will be included.

The Psalms are among the most read, best-loved sections of the Bible. If you pray one psalm per week, starting with "Blessed is the man who does not walk in the counsel of the wicked or stand in the way of sinners" (Ps. 1:1), it would be nearly three years until you would exclaim, "Let everything that has breath praise the Lord. Praise the Lord," (the end of Psalm 150). In between, there is something that pertains to almost every situation in life, whether grieving over a death of the breakup of a marriage or rejoicing in the birth of a baby. Hence, although rooted in particular circumstances, the psalms are timeless. They reveal a dogged faith and great love for God regardless of circumstances, for they are based on God's steadfast love and faithfulness to all generations. These prayers and hymns express a whole rage of human emotion, including anger, sorrow, frustration, and joy. Throughout, the psalmists found a way of giving their unabashed praise for the presence and continuing action of God in their lives, becoming examples to us all.

Not every psalm is represented, but some, such as Psalm 23, with their rich imagery, called for more than one design. As you study each, hopefully you can find something that applies to your situation or that of your faith community, and gives you voice or helps you hear God's voice. Hopefully too you will be inspired to try your hand at interpreting one of the psalms not illustrated here.

Ps. 4:7

For Christians, there is no greater joy than the assurance of salvation. When the weight of sin is lifted, it brings a great sigh of relief and is a time of celebration. To illustrate this passage, I followed my first impulse (often the best kind) and placed a cross, the supreme symbol of salvation, over a heart shape, as in Martin Luther's coat of arms. However, a static cross wouldn't work here, but rather one made of four irregular shapes reaching beyond the heart to the four directions. The other shapes, representing unrestrained joy, add an element of animation. In a sense, this banner becomes an invitation to come to the party. Strictly out of artistic impulse, I chose the present tense as a way of involving the viewer on a more personal level.

Ps. 10:12
Thanksgiving Day

This banner is both a visual prayer requesting God's continuing concern for those among us who feel alone, oppressed, and lacking in resources, and also a call to action. It reminds us of our Christian responsibility to aid others in times of physical or spiritual need.

Ps. 13:6

The New Year, an Anniversary, or Another Reason for Thanksgiving

Certain words or phrases stand alone in their ability to express ideas without graphic design elements. The words in this design are a confident confession, and added lines or geometric shapes would seem out of place. Since this is a visual media, however, the design needs a "spark," something to grab the viewer's attention. Thus, the word *sing* was put in lower case italic to create a subtle focal point for the eye. Also note the progression of colors. As discussed in the opening, a black background causes the colors of the words to pop out, as in a stained-glass window.

BACKGROUND
BLACK (2)

Ps. 16:1

Refuge, shelter, and protection are recurring themes of the psalmists who, like us, experienced times of trial and longed for the sheltering presence of God. In times of distress and peril our faith is a haven, an anchor in a stormy sea. But, how do you express this visually? Focus on your own mental picture of an ideal refuge, some retreat from the troubles of life. It might be hiking on a trail through a portion of God's creation or fishing by a high mountain lake. Shelter is that certain feeling, an island of calm in the midst of chaos, that is portrayed here. The key words, "For in you I take refuge," are placed within a space surrounded by random, chaotic shapes.

The colors are only suggestions. Feel free to chose your own. What colors convey calm? Maybe blue or green? What about distress or impending peril? Try black, gray, or brown as a contrast.

Ps. 19:1

As the psalmist states, the ever changing heavens attest to God's glory. "Day after day they pour forth speech; night after night they display knowledge." Their voice is especially apparent while watching the transition from day to night at sunset. First comes a progression of blues broken by clouds in tints of pink, yellow, orange, and red mixed with mauves and purples. The whole panorama gives way to the deepest of blues and finally to black, painted with a field of stars. Such a passage of time itself becomes a declaration of continuity, gentility, and awesome power—in short, the glory of God.

Outline all the shapes with washable marking pens following the procedure under "Outlining Design Elements" on page 14. Then, to soften the lines, lightly brush over them with plain tap water.

Or, to give the banner a subtle glow, outline all the shapes with flourescent highlighters following the procedure under "Outlining Design Elements" on page 14.

Ps. 23:1
Fourth Sunday of Easter

Psalm 23 is undeniably the most beloved portion of the Bible. Along with John 3:16, more people have committed it to memory than any other passage. The words seem to roll gently off the tongue, like the rippling waters of a high mountain stream. It has provided many a person with comfort in times of anguish and distress. Because the words display a feeling of childlike faith and trust, it is natural to look to the simple drawing style of children for imagery. Young children, especially preschoolers, have the enviable ability to see past unimportant details. The lamb is adapted from a child's drawing, complete with puff-ball body and stick legs.

When all the color areas are in place, complete the banner by using washable marking pens to outline the shapes. A 1/8″ line is best. Use warm colors such as pink, red and orange. For example, outline the shapes for the lamb with pink, the lettering with orange, and the pink and purple shapes (labeled 6, 7, and 25) with red. Then apply a thin coat of tap water over all the washable marking pen lines. This will give the completed banner a softer look.

Ps. 23:2
Fourth Sunday of Easter

The Twenty-third Psalm contains so many rich images that it is hard to stop with one design. Verse 2 calls forth from each of us our vision of an ideal retreat, that place or activity where we can go to "get away from it all" and achieve momentary respite. The psalmist shows us one of those places—by a lake or stream—where one's troubles can get lost in the soft, rhythmic motion and sound of gently moving waters. God, our Shepherd, leads us there and stands by, patient and watchful.

Utilize the washable marking pens outlining technique described on page 14 to outline the water.

Ps. 25:4
Graduation or Confirmation

Psalm 25 is an acrostic. The first letter of each verse follows the order of the 22-letter Hebrew alphabet. This psalm is a prayer by a very troubled person seeking God's guidance and help. When we are troubled by events in our own lives, it is difficult to know whether, as some advise, to "take one day at a time" or to make plans by anticipating the future. If we focus solely on our problems and trials, we may ignore Jesus' advice.

The psalmist's confusion is expressed visually in the irregular shapes leading in four directions (a subtle reminder of the cross) and by the jumble of lettering styles. Rather than making all the lettering in yellow as indicated, you might use a variety of colors culled from materials in your scrap bin.

BACKGROUND
BURGUNDY (4)

LETTERING
YELLOW (12)

Ps. 26:3

As we walked along a high mountain trail on a clear August day, just below timberline, we saw a tree, hundreds of years old, but now almost dead, standing alone atop a ridge, defying the winds and heavy snows that long ago could have knocked it over. That sight spoke volumes about God's loving care, not only for that one tree among billions, but for me as well. Later, as we passed that tree on our way back to our campsite, the setting sun was painting everything with the warm glow of reds and oranges. We saw, again, another subtle reminder of God's everlasting and all-encompassing love.

LETTERING
CRIMSON RED (5)

YOUR LOVE IS EVER BEFORE ME

Ps. 27:1
Holy Week

Words such as besiege, war, and fear, contained in later verses of Psalm 27, inspired the shapes in this design. The visual elements—the shapes and colors—can best be described as 'visual antonyms' to the words which are placed against a field of black, the opposite of light. Daggerlike shapes of impending disaster hover above. It is as if everything were trapped in a deep pit, but God's presence is assured and all fear is vanquished.

This banner is particularly appropriate for Holy Week, especially Maundy Thursday, Good Friday, and/or Holy Saturday. Jesus' journey to the cross is recalled with the full knowledge that Easter is just ahead.

Ps. 30:11

Easter, Times of Special Joy

The sadness of Good Friday disappears in the glow of Easter! In grief the women arrived at the tomb, but leave leaping and dancing for joy. The Lord has answered all our prayers and cries of desperation. If your faith community utilizes the art of dance as a means of conveying the Gospel, and responding to it, then this design is for you.

Ps. 38:21
Lent, Maundy Thursday, Good Friday

Making another appeal to God in a time of distress, the psalmist asks God for companionship. The words take us back momentarily to Gethsemane, recalling Jesus' appeal to his disciples to watch and remain alert. It would therefore be an appropriate visual for Maundy Thursday remembrance, if not during all of Lent.

The lettering on a banner is not just an "add on." Careful attention needs to be paid to the style and positioning of the letters in relation both to the background area and to the other graphic elements. Note how the lettering conveys distance, like a perspective drawing creating an illusion of depth on a two dimensional surface. The other design elements are one person's way of portraying distress and anguish. What "tricks" or graphic elements would you use?

BACKGROUND
BURGUNDY (4)

LETTERING
ORANGE (10)

Ps. 46:10

This psalm inspired Martin Luther's great hymn "A Mighty Fortress Is Our God." This banner makes visible God's reassuring voice, telling us to slow down and realize the joy of his presence.

Ps. 55:17

To this appeal for help, God responds. You can almost hear the sigh of relief!

Ps. 63:7

Shadows. Sometimes they are associated with fear and uncertainty. For other people, shadows are like that grassy place beneath a giant oak, a refuge and a place of security. God, the Holy Spirit shelters us, his young, from the heat and from those who would dare try to snatch us away from God.

Ps. 92:1 (RSV)
Thanksgiving

While the words for this banner are found in verse 1, the graphics were inspired by verse 2 "Declare thy steadfast love in the morning and thy faithfulness by night." The background is halved vertically, the left representing the night; the right, the day. The words, like our expressions of thanks and praise, span both.

Ps. 97:1

Springtime or Harvest

The psalmist raises his voice in proclamation of the power and glory of God. He anthropomorphizes the earth, that is, he gives it human characteristics so that it can respond to God in human terms—an amazing image! It seemed appropriate to use flowers to illustrate the joy of the earth in response to the God who has brought everything into existence.

This design was taken directly from the thumbnail sketch to final form with the aid of a photocopier, the goal being to retain the feeling of freedom and directness of the original rough sketch. The copier was set to its maximum enlargement percentage, and the original pencil sketch was copied onto plain bond paper. Any faint lines were darkened to make them easier to copy. It was then copied on a projection transparency. From there, the design was cast onto a large piece of paper with an overhead projector and traced. Finally, the lines were widened so they could be interpreted in cloth.

Ps. 100:1

Confirmation, Graduation, and Joyful Events

Only five verses long, Psalm 100 comes upon us like a messenger announcing that a great conflict is over and now it is time to party. This design sets the stage visually, because our natural reaction to good news is to shout for joy and sing out with songs of thanksgiving. This design is a visual celebration.

This could be personalized as a confirmation banner by substituting the names of the confirmands for the streamers and other shapes that weave their way through the words.

Ps. 107:1
Thanksgiving

The opening verse of Psalm 107 is heard at the conclusion of many a meal as a way of expressing gratitude for God's continuing gifts. By that same reasoning, it is also appropriate in a worship setting, especially as a visual highlight for Thanksgiving Day.

Ps. 119:76

The length and content of Psalm 119 dictates more than one design. Besides, these words are hard to ignore. As with some of the other designs, the words dominate, but the length of the word *unfailing* required some experimentation. Again, don't be afraid to try something out of the ordinary. Throw in a little surprise, like the heart in the word *love*, to grab the viewer's eye. Another symbol that came to mind in connection with "unfailing love," "comfort" was a flower, the gift of a special friend when the spirits are down. Flowers, a special part of God's creation, express many things, including joy, comfort, beauty, steadfast love, simplicity, grace, and perseverance under pressure. For this design, a single flower becomes a gentle amen. It is placed under the word *comfort*, not to fill an empty space, but to redirect the eye upward. Without it, it might feel as if something is missing.

Ps. 119:105

In this, the longest psalm, the writer uses 176 verses to express an untiring devotion to God's Word. It is "sweeter than honey" (v. 103). It gives meaning to life, sustains in times of difficulty, and becomes, as he says in verse 105, "a light for my (our) path" so that we might see the rough places ahead. With this verse it is hard not to think about Amy Grant's song.

The graphics are derived from a simple photograph taken while hiking a trail through the gently rolling hills of a state park near home. It was early and the sun was beginning to appear on the horizon. Its rays streaked the path ahead, bathing everything ahead in a warm glow, creating a great sense of security. This banner depicts that photograph, border and all.

Ps. 121:2

Psalm 121 belongs to a section of the psalter entitled "Songs of Ascent" (Psalms 120–134). Pilgrims sang these songs as they journeyed to Jerusalem to attend the major religious festivals. You can almost hear their voices echoing off the Judean hills as the celebrants make their way to the temple on Mt. Zion.

Everyone has sleepless nights or mornings when you awaken too early. The more you fight it, the worse it gets. This design came out of one of those experiences: I awoke very early one Saturday morning and turned on the TV to redirect my thought processes. The only shows, other than those ridiculous shopping networks, were cartoons. The images in this design are loosely based on the highly, stylized background shapes in one animated piece that I recorded in a sketch book for future reference. The words of Psalm 121 brought them back to mind.

Ps. 150:6

It is not known if this song was written as a doxology for the book of Psalms, but these words, from the final verse of Psalm 150, make an appropriate amen for this series of banners.

Favorite Hymns

"Abide with Me"
Funeral

Each of us has a special hymn that through the years becomes a kind of personal anthem recalling special events or times of life—a wedding, Baptism, worship experience, or funeral—when that hymn played a memorable role. With its opening bars we remember those events and are overwhelmed with emotion. It becomes difficult to speak, let alone to sing the words. Tears appear at the corner of the eye, there is a tingling in the stomach, or perhaps our mouth turns upward in a faint smile.

This next series takes some of those special creations one step farther by giving them a visual presence. Some of the hymns used are personal favorites, others friends suggested. It is not by words only or music only that a hymn becomes interwoven in our lives. Each is a perfect union of word and music, a marriage.

Certain hymns are memorable because they connect in our memories with singular events early in life. Such a hymn for me is "Abide with Me." It brings to mind a time in grade school when, as part of a children's choir, I sang at the memorial service for a beloved member of the congregation. Every time the fifth verse begins "Hold thou thy cross before my closing eyes …" my eyes swell and turn red. My singing becomes faint, almost inaudible, except to God, who hears it as a quiet, personal prayer.

"Amazing Grace! How Sweet the Sound"
Reformation

One of the most beautiful and beloved of all hymns, written by former slave trader, John Newton, "Amazing Grace! How Sweet the Sound" is a poetic extension of St. Paul's words in Eph. 2:8–9 "For it is by grace you have been saved, through faith—not by works."

The irregular crosses behind the words visually tie the design together and serve as a reminder of the instrument of God's grace.

"Beautiful Savior"
Funeral

"Beautiful Savior," like "Amazing Grace! How Sweet the Sound," is a perfect union of words and melody. It is unfortunate that the author is unknown, because credit should be given to someone for this magical creation. It is almost as if an angel gave it to us as a gift. As this hymn is sung, it creates a feeling of gentle waves flowing from one person to another, creating a sense of security and well-being.

The images are adapted from a cloth sample I kept in a notebook for future reference. Only three colors are used: red for the background, white for the flowers, and black for the lines.

Follow this procedure:

1. Cast the images directly onto white cloth and trace all lines with a colored pencil (see recommendations under "Marking Tools," p. 7).

2. After bonding the lettering and flowers to the background, retrace all the pencil lines with a medium black permanent felt-tip marking pen. For the flowers, use a ⅛" to ³⁄₁₆" line; for the lettering, a thin (¹⁄₁₆") outline is best.

"What a Friend We Have in Jesus"

Valentine's Day, the Epiphany Season

When I began working on this series, I polled several people to find out which hymns were their personal favorites. This design was developed in response to a request by one of my closest and dearest friends who told me that one of her fondest childhood memories was of those times when her grandmother involved her in impromptu hymn sings during long family automobile trips. One of her grandmother's favorites was "What a Friend We Have in Jesus." As they sang, they would clap their hands, and their bodies would sway back and forth to the gentle cadence. Soon everyone joined in. Even the scenery seemed to roll past the windows in time to their rhythm. What a great memory to carry through life!

The symbols in this design are simple—a heart, signifying love, and a cross, the reminder of Jesus' loving action. What a friend, indeed!

"Lord, Dismiss Us with Your Blessing"

Traditionally this hymn is sung at the close of worship as a musical benediction. It serves to set a positive tone for the beginning of a new week.

One of the greatest challenges in creating a banner is finding the right words. They must express a feeling or mood with inspiring images to set the imagination soaring. These words brought to mind a wild vision of flying hearts moving in graceful harmony through the heavens.

LETTERING
LT. BLUE (18)

BACKGROUND
MAGENTA (24)

"Lift High the Cross"
Sundays of Easter

This is a superb post-Easter hymn. Christ's rising from the tomb defeated the power of sin and transformed the cross from symbolizing defeat to standing for ultimate victory. No more an object of ridicule, the cross now leads the way to triumph.

"O Little Town of Bethlehem"

Christmas

This banner was inspired by one of the most beloved of all Christmas songs. The caption, from stanza 4, speaks a gentle prayer for an inner peace that comes from the knowledge of Christ's presence in our lives.

The format is in the style of tapestries and woven rugs from the United States' Southwest region, and it is especially adaptive for representing hymns and psalms containing multiple images. In planning this design, the background was randomly divided into horizontal bands of color in varying widths to serve as spaces in which to arrange abstract images pulled from the hymn's stanzas. For example, a star and adobelike buildings represent the town itself. Don't be afraid to change some symbols to conform with your vision of Christmas. For example, place a couple of small angels in the sixth band down from the top, or substitute small stars for the row of circles. In other words, indulge your whims and have fun.

"When I Survey the Wondrous Cross"
Easter Sunrise

This hymn opens with a view of the cross on Easter morning, and that is the point of view of this design, with the sun rising behind.

"My Hope Is Built on Nothing Less"

I once overheard someone exclaim, "That hymn really gives me a lift." As the melody rises, it is almost as if it had wings to carry us upward for a view of everything from a different perspective. The design called for something obvious as a visual—a giant rock, perhaps the cornerstone of a building, inscribed with the words. The little rocks floating around it add visual interest and depth.

A thin outline of each rock with a black marker may be all that is needed to give this design a subtle zing.

"Lord, Take My Hand and Lead Me"

Classified under the heading of Christian Hope, this hymn is a simple but eloquent prayer for God's guidance. It speaks with the voice of a child, in the overall tone of Psalm 23. Inspiration was drawn from Michelangelo's painting of the creation of Adam on the ceiling of the Sistine Chapel, where God reaches out to touch Adam with the gift of life. As with Adam, God's extended hand reaches out to us.

"Earth and All Stars"
Labor Day

Written for the 90th anniversary of St. Olaf College in 1964, this hymn uses symbols contemporary to our time, along with unconventional, almost outlandish adjectives; e.g., "loud rushing planets," "loud boiling test tubes." God is manifested in all aspects of daily life and our greatest expression of praise is the way we perform our daily tasks.

"How Great Thou Art"

Like many popular hymns, "How Great Thou Art" was inspired by nature. Its author, Carl Gustaf Boberg (1859–1940), while returning from a meeting in the still of the evening, was struck by the beauty of nature combined with the sound of church bells.

The format and style of the design is based on native American weavings. Versatile and fun, it is a good method to use if the creative juices seem slow.

To try something similar, divide your background into horizontal rectangular areas, not necessarily of the same width. Separating them with thin colored bands adds visual interest and further unifies the design. Next, read through the stanzas of your chosen hymn or Bible passage or whatever excited your imagination, noting the visual images. Cut out abstract shapes representing those visual images, using a variety of colored cloth pieces. Then, by trial and error, arrange the pieces within the rectangular areas until you achieve a pleasing arrangement. Then bond or glue the shapes into place. Another design utilizing a similar format is found on p. 81.

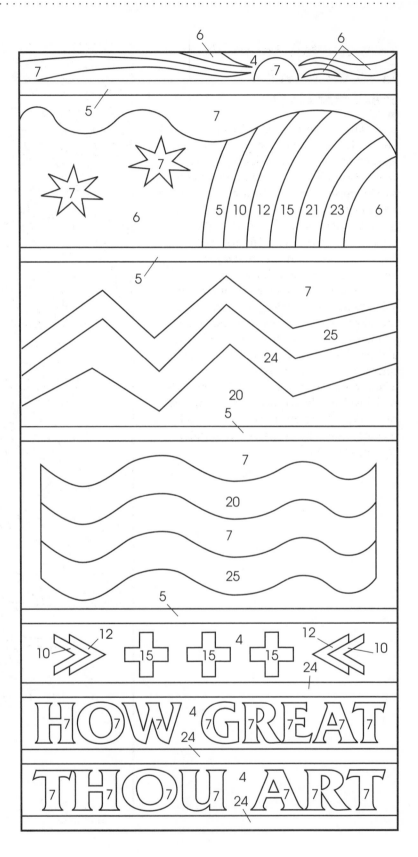

"Immortal, Invisible, God Only Wise"
Pentecost Season

The hymns of Walter Chalmers Smith (1824–1908) have been described as "rich in thought and vigorous in expression." The powerful opening phrases of this hymn speak in no uncertain terms of the presence of God.

This design was inspired by the phrase "We blossom and flourish like leaves on a tree, and wither and perish, but naught changeth thee" in stanza 3. It brought to mind the glorious but all too brief display of fall color when leaves are transformed into miniature stained glass windows. Our lives like leaves, are fragile and brief. The bright chartreuse greens of spring usher in the deep greens of summer. Then come the yellows, oranges, and reds of fall which all too quickly disappear with the winds and colds of winter. But God remains constant throughout: immortal, invisible, awesome!

LETTERING
YELLOW (12)

BACKGROUND
FOREST GREEN (16)

Eyewitnesses of Jesus' Passion

This series brings us face to face with some of the well-known and sometimes notorious people who were involved in Jesus' suffering and death. Each design invites us to feel their emotions and to read their thoughts. The series can be executed entirely with cloth, but it will work best if painted.

Materials

- 2 1/2 to 3 yds. white or off-white fabric (poplin, trigger cloth, or similar with smooth texture)

- 1 qt. flat black latex paint

- 2 fl. oz. tube of artist's acrylic paint in crimson red or dark red

- 2 (ea.) natural bristle brushes, 1" to 1 1/2" wide (for large areas) and 1/4" wide (for details and lettering)

- Miscellaneous items necessary for finishing: overhead projector, masking tape, Stitch Witchery, straight pins, no. 2 pencils, a small plastic container for mixing paint

- A large, smooth, flat work area, ideally a clean garage floor or a sheet of plywood

Procedure

- Pick a finished size for the banners (3 × 6 or 4 × 8, for example) and trim cloth to size adding 3/4" to the sides and bottom, and 3" to the top for finishing.

- Stabilize sides and bottom edge (see steps 1–3 under "Lining Method III," p. 13), then add a pole casing to the top (see "Finishing the Top Edge," p. 14). Add drapery weights to bottom corners to prevent curling of bottom edge when hanging. Copy the designs from this book onto projection transparencies.

- Tape prepared background cloth to wall at eye level. Turn on projector and cast design onto cloth, squaring the image to the edges.

- Trace face and lettering with no. 2 pencil.

- Be sure all elements are traced, then place cloth on work surface. Paint face details with the black paint. Use the 1"–1 1/2" brush for broad areas and the 1/4" brush for fine details.

- Paint lettering with crimson red or dark red artist's acrylic and 1/4" brush. Thin slightly with water for right consistency. A certain amount of roughness adds spontaneity.

- Allow to dry thoroughly before handling.

Optional: Lettering can be completed using cloth and fusible web or glue for bonding. If this is your choice, trace the lettering separately onto paper to make a pattern. Proceed as outlined in "Putting the Banner Together" (see p. 10).

These designs are most effective when used in conjunction with meditations based on the Gospel accounts.

Jesus in Gethsemane
Matt. 26:38

The Passion journey first takes us across the Kidron Valley from Jerusalem to the slopes of the Mount of Olives, to a small orchard where olives were pressed to extract their oil. Hence comes the name Gethsemane, which means the garden of the oilpress. Jesus came here often for prayer and restoration, but that night was different. He had come to these familiar surroundings for the last time, not to rest, but to prepare himself for his work of redemption.

Upon entering the garden, eight of Jesus' disciples waited near the gate. Jesus with three disciples, James, John and Peter, went a little farther. Jesus was deep in thought, but after a few moments he spoke: " 'My soul is overwhelmed with sorrow to the point of death. Stay here and keep watch with me.' Going a little farther, he fell with his face to the ground and prayed, 'My Father, if it's possible, may this cup be taken from me. Yet not as I will, but as you will.' Then he returned to his disciples and found them sleeping. 'Could you men not keep watch with me for one hour?' he asked Peter. 'Watch and pray so that you will not fall into temptation.' " A second and a third time he went off to pray, and again found his disciples sleeping. " 'Are you still sleeping and resting? Look, the hour is near, and the Son of Man is betrayed into the hands of sinners. Rise, let us go! Here comes my betrayer!' " (Matt. 26:38–46).

Judas Betrays Jesus
Luke 22:47

We return to the road leading from Jerusalem to the Mount of Olives. That night a large crowd armed with clubs and swords had gathered on the road, among them Judas, one of Jesus' disciples. Earlier that evening Judas had been with Jesus and his friends for the Passover meal. But Jesus, well aware of Judas's plans, after some very frank words dismissed Judas before he could finish eating. Judas had agreed to identify Jesus in the dark: "The one I kiss is the man; arrest him."

The name Judas is synonymous with betrayal. Someone once said that if it weren't for Judas, the whole show would not have gone on in the first place. That statement shows a note of ignorance. The Jewish officials had already decided to rid themselves of Jesus and the controversy he presented. In their determination, they would have found a way to follow through on their plan. Judas, under the influence of Satan, came out of anonymity and made it easier. For 30 pieces of silver, the price of a slave, he led them to the place where Jesus could be seized quietly. When he approached, Jesus asked him, "Judas, are you betraying the Son of Man with a kiss?" (Luke 22:48).

During the next hour Judas watched as Jesus was shuttled from one period of questioning to another. His emotions raging with anger, remorse, and confusion, he returned the 30 pieces of silver to the chief priests. "I have sinned, for I have betrayed innocent blood" (Matt. 27:4). "I have sinned," he kept repeating to himself. In his mind there was only one way out.

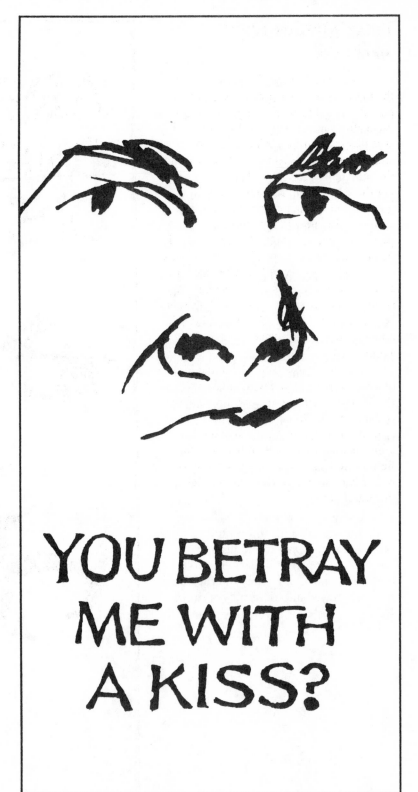

Peter Denies Jesus
Mark 14:70

We move next to the courtyard of the high priest's palace where the Sanhedrin had gathered that night in an unusual after-hours session. All the top officials had met with the high priests Annas and Caiaphas to consider the fate of Jesus, the Nazarene. Peter, who had been watching the events from a distance, joined a group of people who were standing around a fire outside the high priest's palace to stave off the chill in the night air. As he stood there "one of the servant girls of the high priest came by. When she saw Peter warming himself, she looked closely at him. 'You also were with that Nazarene, Jesus,' she said. But he denied it. 'I don't know or understand what you're talking about'" (Mark 14:66–68).

This design portrays the initial look of astonishment mixed with anger on Peter's face when the servant girl confronted him. He thought he could quietly melt into the crowd, but there was something in his manner that made him stand out. Besides, Jesus had earlier predicted what would happen, for Jesus could see right through Peter.

Jesus before Pilate
John 18:38 (RSV)

Now we enter the palace where early that Friday the Roman governor, Pontius Pilate, sat alone, pondering the fate of the itinerant teacher from Nazareth, Jesus. Nobody wanted anything to do with him, that was clear. The Jewish officials were impatient to get rid of him, though unwilling to handle the matter themselves. Pilot had earlier asked them to recount Jesus' crimes, but they responded, "If he were not a criminal, we would not have handed him over to you." Wanting to hand Jesus back to them, Pilate continued, "Take him yourselves and judge him by your own law." They objected, "We have no right to execute anyone" (John 18:30–31).

Then there was the matter of that message Pilate had received from his wife: "Don't have anything to do with that innocent man, for I have suffered a great deal today in a dream because of him" (Matt. 27:19). Through all of this Jesus had said nothing to indict himself. Finally, Pilate reached a decision, of sorts. It was customary every year at Passover to release a prisoner. "I'll give them a choice between Jesus and the convicted insurrectionist and murderer, Barabbas. Surely they will pick Jesus," thought Pilate, "and I can wash my hands of this whole affair." Of course, it didn't turn out like that.

I FIND NO CRIME IN HIM

Simon of Cyrene
A Face in the Crowd

By camel or on foot, Simon, a devout Jew from Cyrene on the north coast of Africa, had made the long journey to Jerusalem to attend the Feast of the Passover. We can only guess his thoughts upon arriving. No doubt he recalled the psalmist's description of the city: "It is beautiful in its loftiness, the joy of the whole earth" (Ps. 48:2), as he eagerly anticipated his visit to the temple.

Upon entering the city, Simon noticed a procession from one of the city gates. Curiosity drew him nearer, to see three men straining under the 30 or 40 pounds of wooden beams across their shoulders. Yet another crucifixion! Placards carried by soldiers announced their crimes. One placard, carried in front of a man wearing a crown of thorns on his head, read simply, "King of the Jews." Simon watched this "king" struggle under his burden. He looked weak and his back was whipped to a bloody pulp! Apparently the officer in charge did not believe that this "king," Jesus, could carry his beam all the way to their destination.

"You there! Take his place," the soldier called.

Simon searched the crowd around him, thinking, "Who's he calling?"

The soldier grabbed Simon and said gruffly, "You, carry this cross for him." Dark thoughts raced through Simon's mind. "Why me? The humiliation! To come here and be treated like the worst kind of criminal. What have I done to deserve this?" But he simply had no choice. It was God's will too that he bear our Savior's cross. Over the last 20 centuries many a pilgrim has looked at Simon with envy while remembering Jesus' words, "If anyone would come after me, he must deny himself and take up his cross and follow me" (Matt. 16:24). Simon was privileged. He had been accorded the greatest of honors!

Mary, Jesus' Mother
John 19:26–27

Finally, we stand at the skull-shaped hill along one of the roads leading away from Jerusalem. In Latin, it was called Calvary; in Aramaic, Golgotha. Three men hung from crosses that Friday. The sight was so commonplace that passersby hardly seemed to notice. There was not much anyone could do for them anyhow, except to take pity on them and curse the Romans.

A small group was keeping vigil there at Calvary. Among them were one of Jesus' disciples and several women, including Jesus' mother. You can imagine her thoughts as she watched her Son struggling to breathe. She saw the lifeblood literally drain from his body. If only his ordeal would end quickly. Jesus saw his mother standing nearby and spoke to her. "Dear woman, here is your son," he said, referring to the disciple, John. To the disciple he said, "Here is your mother" (John 19:26–27). Even as he died, Jesus' compassion for the plight of others was evident.